BITTEN BY A CAMEL

BITTEN BY A CAMEL

LEAVING CHURCH, FINDING GOD

KENT DOBSON

FORTRESS PRESS

MINNEAPOLIS

BITTEN BY A CAMEL
Leaving Church, Finding God

Cover image: Mariia Savoskula, shutterstock.com
Cover design: Brad Norr
Author photo: Brian Kelly Photography and Film

Hardcover ISBN: 978-1-5064-1774-5
eBook ISBN: 978-1-5064-1775-2

The paper used in this publication meets the minimum
requirements of American National Standard for Information
Sciences — Permanence of Paper for Printed Library Materials,
ANSI Z329.48-1984.
Manufactured in the U.S.A.

This book was produced using Pressbooks.com, and PDF
rendering was done by PrinceXML.

CONTENTS

ACKNOWLEDGMENTS

I am deeply grateful to my family who has weathered the ups and downs of my own wild spiritual undoing. My kids have kept things light, helping me not take all this spiritual talk, or myself, too seriously. My wife has waited patiently, farther down the road, letting me work things out in my own time. I could not have written this book or gone on my little adventures without her concern, care, support and challenging questions. Tony Jones and Doug Pagitt invited me to speak at a Christianity 21 event where I first started thinking about the camel story and speaking publicly about what was no longer working for me. Without the invitation, this book wouldn't have been born. Tony later became my editor and took me out to the woodshed more than once, for which I am really thankful. And thanks to Rob Bell for helping me see the outline of the book one afternoon and inspiring me to keep going.

1

SPIRITUAL MOUNTAINEERING

What made Mount Sinai so alluring to me was the story that God and human beings once made contact in this place. God broke the silence between us. Though I didn't admit it to anyone, I wanted that silence to be broken again. I hoped that my earnest searching for God would pay off, just a little bit.

At the same time, I was unsure of what I actually believed about God. I wanted to hear—or experience—something real. So I tried to silence my questions and turned in good will toward the Sinai desert.

I was a twenty-eight-year-old grad student living in Jerusalem on a weeklong field study for class through Egypt and the Sinai Peninsula. The class ended with a night climb to the top of Mount Sinai for the sunrise. It's an amazingly stark and beautiful place. The Sinai Peninsula is one of the most pristine and untouched biblical landscapes left on earth. In this barren wilderness stands the mountain where

God gave Moses the Ten Commandments, the mountain where God's dark and fiery presence came to rest in a cloud of mystery.

I could not think of a more inspired place to ask God for direction in my life. I needed help. I was anxious and uncertain about the future. I'd been leading worship music at a wildly successful megachurch called Mars Hill Bible Church in Grand Rapids, Michigan before moving to Jerusalem with my wife and eighteen-month-old daughter for school. The desire to find out what the Bible *really* said and to search for the historical Jesus had inspired me to make the move. But now that my studies were coming to an end, I didn't know what to do with myself or what was best for the family. I wondered if I should stay on the academic path in Israel or go back to work in a church.

I'm not sure exactly what kind of answer I expected from God on the top of the mountain. I didn't need stone tablets from heaven—just a hint, a nudge, a clue about what to do with my life, or even a suggestion about what really matters in this world. I kept thinking about Elijah who heard a "still, small voice" when he came to Sinai in search of God.

Part of me hoped that God had a special plan for me, that God was working out some secret divine math behind the scenes. This is what I was taught about the way God works: "I know the plans I have for you declares the Lord, plans to make you prosper and not to harm you." Never mind this passage in Jeremiah is about the ancient nation of Israel. As evangelicals—the tribe in which I was raised—we understood it individually and personally. It was risky to move to the Middle East, more so than I ever knew when we boarded the plane, so I was really hoping there was a divine plan. And if it wasn't a clearly defined plan, a little assurance that my life had some greater purpose would be just fine.

I'd moved to Israel without a career goal. I squirmed and struggled to answer when one of my professors asked me, "What's your professional plan?" I made something up about writing historical fiction, which he called, "Interesting." But I was actually just curious about faith—my own faith, Christian faith in the Bible, and whether I really believed it all. Although I'd been raised inside the evangelical church—deep inside—I knew very little about the history of my own tradition or the Bible we cherished so much. And now I was about to graduate with a master's degree in biblical history and geography. I figured this piece of paper was going to serve me about as well as my undergrad degree in English. I sincerely wanted to ask God if I should stay in Israel for more schooling or go back home to the church, a world about which I felt increasingly confused.

On the overnight train from Aswan, I read the Sinai account in the Torah very carefully. Crammed into the top of a bunk bed, without enough room to sit upright, I stared at this 3,000-year-old story, hunting for clues. According to the book of Exodus, Moses instructed the Israelites to "deny themselves." I knew from my Jewish studies that this was interpreted as a requirement to fast. I laid down on my back and looked at the smoke-stained train ceiling. I wanted to be as prepared as the Israelites in case of any divine messages. So I decided to fast from that point on, quietly, as good Christians are supposed to do.

SEARCHING FOR GOD IN THE PROMISED LAND

In Israel, away from my church and my parents, I felt a new-found freedom to doubt out loud, to wonder, to question the way I felt about God. A lot of my faith had stopped making sense, and so had a lot of church stuff. I was tired of my worn-out belief system, the one I was supposed to hold. It was like searching for some spiritual country that I'd heard rumors about.

Life in Jerusalem was just the ticket out of my old life; except it wasn't the nice spiritual homecoming that tourists talk about. I've heard many Christian visitors say that when they stepped off the plane, they just knew they were "home." My dad said this when he first visited Israel—as the story goes, he even got down on his hands and knees and kissed the tarmac. But for me, it wasn't a homecoming. It was a struggle: trying to pay my bills at the post office; negotiating a rental agreement; going to the mall to pick up my army-issued gas mask.

If you want to be shaken to your core, if you want to eat amazing food, if you want to unlearn all your political positions, if you want to marvel at the complexity and beauty and ridiculousness of religious expression, if you want your faith to fall apart, if you want to stand in awe while waiting for the bus, if you want to barter in the market the old-fashioned way, if you want to be at the center of the world's psycho-spiritual upheaval, then Jerusalem is your place.

One night a teenager with a suicide belt blew up Café Hillel, just down the street from my apartment. Hillel felt like *my* café, on *my* street, where I shopped and ate and met friends and brought my kids. Seven people were killed. A father and daughter died while sharing a meal; she was to be married the next day.

I felt the blast as I was working on a paper for class. I had never felt such terror, crawling all over my body. Moments later I was in the street, with the spin of emergency lights, and the shouts of Orthodox Jewish EMTs, their side curls bouncing on their shoulders. A water pipe had burst in a garden across the street, showering the asphalt like it was trying to wash away the terror.

The shock of the bombing unearthed a lot of my own internal hurt and fear, which I'd been trying hard to ignore—fear that was rooted in questions about the arbitrariness of life, questions that flew in the face of my evangelical upbringing: Some people get married. Others do not. Some people happen to sit in the wrong seat at the wrong time in the wrong place. Some people get sick. Some people get ALS like my dad, others do not. That very night I had considered texting my friend Matt to see if he wanted to grab a late-night coffee at Café Hillel. But texting on a flip phone is annoying, so I stayed in.

In that moment, shivering in the dark, I knew that God didn't cause this madness—if God existed at all. God did not even "allow" this random act of violence, as Christians like me are prone to say. This was not "God's will." And God could not stop it. *There was no plan.* There was no man upstairs. I could no longer believe in a puppeteer God pulling the strings of circumstance. The pizza place next door turned the suicide bomber away, so he just walked to the next crowded restaurant. That's the way it is. Totally arbitrary. Random.

Something was collapsing inside me, and it had been for a long time before that night on Emek Refiam in West Jerusalem, the night the café was bombed. And whatever it was couldn't be put back together again. But I didn't have words for what was falling apart. I didn't want it to fall apart. I wanted my faith to grow. But even more, I wanted my family to be safe. I wanted to be alive and do normal things. I hated looking for the safest seat in a café, or holding my breath when a bus passed by, or constantly sizing up who was Jewish and who was Palestinian, a skill I had mastered.

Café Hillel, and Jerusalem, and all my studies and confusion were with me on the way to Sinai, on the way to find out what it all meant, on the way to meet a God who didn't seem to exist, on the way to a mountain where a divine, biblical encounter may or may not have happened.

I was desperate for some kind of answer. But I wasn't sure if I was asking good questions anymore.

I also wanted to pray, even though I had a whole history of failing to pray in any consistent way that felt real. In my pocket was a Hebrew-English version of the Psalms. It had the look of wisdom and depth. I said these short Hebrew prayers in the ancient language, as genuinely as I could, through my doubts and my struggle to understand the words.

When I first moved to Israel, I flirted with converting to Judaism. My head was full Chaim Potok novels and Abraham Heschel quotes. I loved the Jewish embrace of questions. And unlike my own faith tradition, the practices didn't feel like they were made up in the 1970s. What would Jesus *really* do, I wondered? He was Jewish, after all.

My Orthodox landlord was like a rabbi to me. He took me to his synagogue on the Sabbath and we talked about the Torah when I dropped off my rent. One night he picked me up in his tiny Ford and told me to bring a *kippah* (also known as a *yarmulke*) and wear a white shirt. We drove to an Ultraorthodox neighborhood a few blocks away. The Jewish festival of Sukkot was in full swing, the only festival where the Bible commands the participants to celebrate with joy. Next thing I knew, I was dancing with Russian Jews in striped coats, holding hands with strangers, sweat pouring down my face. My landlord kept smiling and laughing, like we had a great secret. Surely I was the only Gentile in the room, and probably one of only a few to be a part of this world, if only for a night. My heart swelled with the music as we spun in circles till we were both exhausted.

But ultimately, I was just a visitor. Judaism is an ethnicity and a culture, not just a religion, not something I could just sign up for like a class. As my respect for Judaism rose, my heartfelt desire to be one of the "chosen people" diminished. Trying to join another faith seemed a little crazy after a night of dancing to Yiddish songs and trying to keep my *kippah* from falling off my head. When I got back to my apartment, drums still ringing in my ears, I could feel my own growing religious homelessness, even as the joy of this totally insane night made me smile.

BEDOUIN LAND ROVERS

The day or so leading up to Sinai I spent occasionally praying, hiding my hunger, reading the Torah, and otherwise killing time. My inner state of mind was probably the real issue, but Egypt felt a little depressing and dirty, with a lot of mangy cats. One of the oldest civilizations on earth was selling every kind of cheap tourist trinket at every stop. I longed to get away from the Nile and into the Sinai Peninsula. When we finally entered the Sinai Desert by bus, our professor announced that he had arranged a great surprise: we were going through the wilderness, not by bus or camel, but by Land Rover. The Bedouin would be our guides, their ancient faces our maps of the desert.

Happy with the thought of adventure, we crammed into the back of two old Land Rovers, facing one another on bench seats. The Bedouin were all smiles and cigarette smoke as we set off on our biblical trek. The first fifteen minutes were wildly exciting as we jerked and swayed on sand and rocks, over only the faintest signs of a road. We took turns gripping the ceiling and bracing for the next bump. But then a sixty-year-old student who was auditing the course hit her head on the ceiling. Our enthusiasm waned. She looked frightened and hurt. The Bedouin were giving us the thumbs up, smiling and lighting more cigarettes. After an hour at speeds near forty-five miles an hour, we started hating our professor and the evil Bedouin.

Because our Land Rover was second in this convoy of torture, we were also inhaling dust. I cursed the Bedouin, the Sinai, and my empty stomach. I felt like a child of the nation of Israel, bitching to Moses about the liberation of the wilderness, longing to go back to slavery in Egypt.

Two hours later we stumbled out of the vehicles. We were at an ancient Egyptian mining site, a long-forgotten archeological blah, blah, blah. Sinai was still a long way off. The Bedouins' bread and tea were a welcome sight, except that I was now super-spiritual and couldn't eat. I spent lunch regretting my newfound religious discipline, but I managed to avoid eating without making a scene.

I poked around for the road to the bus, but alas, one more surprise: we would be taking the Land Rovers all the way to the hotel next to Mount Sinai. Bloody hell. As the miles bumped by, we took turns talking about food and lamenting the whole trip. As nightfall descended and the hotel came into view, after hours of spine-rattling abuse, all we could talk about was food. My classmates went straight into the dining hall like wild dogs. Some were hugging; one person was crying.

I left my personal religious devotion back in the Land Rover. I not only went straight to the buffet, but also started eating while in line. If I was a religious failure, I might as well embrace it. Maybe I could make amends on the way up the mountain. I ate till I was stuffed, and then I wandered back to my hotel room, deflated and sore. I turned over in my bed restlessly till the alarm went off at 3:30am to start the climb.

CLIMBING THE MOUNTAIN OF GOD

It was clear and cold, as the desert should be. The stars were close. The path was primitive, as if Moses had cleared it. I felt alive this cold night, looking into the darkness and the unknown. I imagined a silent pilgrimage to the summit. My head was full of monks and prayer books and the heart-felt undertow of adventure. Within a few hundred yards I heard, "Camel ride, camel ride." The Bedouin were back. I shrugged off the first few offers with condescending swagger. But they kept coming, "It's too far. Camel ride. You, my friend, Camel ride." I put my head down in resolve and passed through their clouds of smoke in the night air.

I remembered that the Torah said to put a perimeter around the mountain so that no animal could ascend. Suddenly I was a fundamentalist wanting to enforce the rules, "Haven't you read the text, you hypocrites?" I wondered. I tried to shake it off. But as I continued, I realized that I was not alone, and the Bedouin were just the beginning. The trail was crowded with Russian women in high-heels, Asian tourists laughing and posing for photos, and the spiritually lazy riding camels.

It was cold and getting colder. I felt a growing solitude as I climbed. I wondered what I was doing with my life. I started thinking about God and Jesus. What was this whole thing anyway? What was I searching for? My classmates receded into the night. The climb was hard. I sweated through my thin layers. The cold began to break me down. Sinai was more difficult than I expected.

I began shivering, then shaking, getting nervous. I imagined what hypothermia did to the body. I'd forgotten about my lonely pilgrimage of prayer. I paused again to catch my breath, rubbing my arms to stay warm, and looked down at my feet. In the crag of a rock I saw some fabric, dusty and trampled. I reached down and grabbed a ski hat. How lucky! Maybe Aaron had worn it. Even in the moonlight I could see that it was filthy. I shook it off and put it on my head, glancing around to see if anyone noticed how little shame I had. The dust settled on my eyebrows. I was feeling more and more defeated, less and less spiritual, wondering what on earth I was doing up here.

After a couple of hours of climbing, the summit appeared ahead. Of course, just below the final climb were Bedouin tents, their generators humming, an encampment of comfort for the fools who had made the climb. I blinked a few times, as if this might be a dream, which it wasn't. I went straight into a tent, bought a hot chocolate, and ate a Snickers bar. I felt like a spiritual slob. What an opportunity I had been given. But I felt like a waste, like a spiritual waste. I sat in the tent with a few of my fellow students. We all felt a little strange in the pre-dawn of this holy site, in a tent with tourists from all over the world.

When I began to thaw, my good spiritual thoughts returned. I remembered that I wanted desperately for God to make sense of my life. I headed out to the summit with a few classmates, and I wised up. For $10, I rented a nasty, camel-scented blanket from a Bedouin. I wrapped it around myself and sat just below the strange crowd gathering in this dark wilderness. And I waited.

It was vast, this ocean of silence and rock. In that moment, it did not matter to me if this was the real Sinai or if the biblical events really happened here, or happened at all. The desert was real. I wondered how this expanse of quiet harshness had birthed Israel, the Bible, and maybe even God.

The rounded granite mountaintops lit up first, like a creeping orange fire. The world was being born. It was the first day of creation. The sun came over the horizon. I felt the first real warmth on my face in the last four hours. A swell of tears started in my chest. I heard quiet voices beginning to sing, a hymn perhaps to the waking up of eternity and time. It grew louder. I recognized the song. It was the Beatles, "Here Comes the Sun." Seriously?

Who are these people? What the hell is going on?

The crowd began to clap and cheer like we had just won something. The hillside was full, hundreds of people, from all over the world, happy to be alive and to cheer on the sun. My personal questions faded for a moment. I forgot all about my search for the meaning of my own life. What had this ghost, Moses, started 3,000 years ago? Were we all here for the same thing, all wondering what the point of life is, all looking for some guidance, a plan, a hint, a message, a word, a whisper, some peace, well-being, happiness, warmth? And just now, we were happy to be alive and to be warm. Here we were, in awe of the endless ocean of silent hills coming into the light.

As the crowd dispersed, I climbed onto an outcropping of stone and took out my book of Psalms. I tried to read a few. Then I asked God what I should do with my life, what was next, what direction to walk. I closed my eyes. I prayed. I wondered. I prayed again. I waited. I felt silly. There was a lot of silence, no sign, no divine word, no guidance, no rush of clarity. My studies were coming to a close—this I knew, but not much else.

When I opened my eyes, I felt small. For a moment, it was like I could feel my actual life, without all of my theological filters or ideas or even questions. I was just a guy on a hillside in the desert holding a rented blanket and book of psalms. When I look back now, I know that my actual life was not lining up with my supposed beliefs, that a rupture had developed between them. At the time, however, I couldn't see this rift. But it was going to change my life.

I could also feel my fingers again. I'd grown fond of my nasty hat. I looked around, thinking I would never be up here again, and wondering how I ever ended up here in the first place. I returned the blanket and headed down the mountain. I thought that my Sinai adventure was over.

CAMEL TEETH

I came around a bend and saw a camel, resting from his night of forced labor. People were walking past and carrying on with their business. As I walked by, the camel reached out, opened his massive mouth, and lunged toward my face. Like a ninja, I blocked his attack with my arm. But now my elbow was in the back of his throat. His rotting teeth were inches from my chin and digging into my upper arm. I could feel his hot breath on my face. He began to yank like a dog with a chew toy.

I looked around desperately for someone to help me. There was no one. I released a flood of expletives. I yelled things that have never been uttered on Mount Sinai. I broke all the commandments.

The only solution I could think of in my panic was to punch the camel in the face. I reached back with my free arm, and started to swing. But with prophetic vision, I suddenly imagined a Bedouin leaping on my back, his curved knife in hand, ready to slit my throat, screaming, "Don't touch my camel!" I hesitated. The camel let go.

We stood face-to-face and eye-to-eye. I was looking into his massive, black pupils. Then he took a short breath and blew snot all over my face. The whole world stopped spinning. It was perfectly still. We had both ceased to breathe. There was no noise. Then I took a breath and felt my arm. I checked to see if my elbow was still working and calmly backed away. I stood there in shock for a moment, and then turned away. I resumed walking down the trail, totally bewildered and in pain.

Now seriously, why did I climb this mountain? I wondered. What was I even doing up here—I mean *really* doing? I didn't know.

In fact, it took me a long time to even admit to others

or myself what had happened on my spiritual quest. I didn't know if I could make sense of it, or if it was even something worth trying to make sense of. But the story would not go away. Sinai kept flashing up when I least expected it. Sometimes I wondered if it really even happened. The more I tried to make sense of it, the more elusive it seemed. For the first few months, I only told a couple of people. When I finally told an Israeli friend of mine a few years later, he laughed so hard that he cried. Every time I see him he tries to get me to tell him the story again. He begs. He tried to pay me 100 shekels to tell a group he was guiding, just so he could laugh.

But for a moment, in the morning light of Sinai, with saliva on my jacket and pain in my arm, I knew there was no right path. I knew there was no clear plan, not like I'd hoped. Whatever I was looking for was utterly unlike what I was looking for. I'd been reduced to just being me, faults, hang-ups, misgivings, desires, dirty clothes, and doubts. I was only myself, and to be frank, I barely knew what it was like to be me. In all my earnest devotion, I was trying to get away from myself, or fix myself, or make myself believe something, or do enough righteous stuff to find myself, and also to find God.

What happened to me on Sinai? It's hard to say. It was the start of something, and the ending of something. Being bitten by a camel closed some hard-to-name door, and it helped get new things going. Coming down the mountain was the start of something more difficult—a fruitful darkness that is more expansive than I had ever thought possible.

On Sinai, I didn't find the God I was looking for. I descended the mountain as an utter spiritual failure, unable to fast, unable to pray, unable to say what I believed, unsure of the Bible. But it was the start of a new faith journey, though I didn't know that at the time. Jerusalem and Sinai were metaphors for what was happening in me. I went out to find something over there, in a special place, but that something never showed up, not in any way I could recognize. I couldn't find God in the most holy place on earth. So I had to stumble back home and say, "I don't know." This was all the enlightenment I could muster.

A WINDING ROAD

My family and I moved back to Michigan shortly after my Sinai debacle. I thought maybe it would all make sense soon enough, but I had a hard time finding a job and adjusting to America. It didn't feel much like a new chapter, in part, because we rented my childhood home from my parents. I pitched a job to Mars Hill Bible Church, which I pretty much invented, only to be flatly rejected. I hoped to bring back to the church the volumes of biblical stuff I'd amassed in a short period of time. This was a blow. Why had I gone to Israel? I wondered. I delivered phone books to make ends meet. Then I went to the hospital, without insurance, with a "non-specific stomach ailment." I also got shingles, which really, really hurt. So we left Michigan for Georgia and I started working for my father-in-law as a (pretty poor) carpenter. I broke as many tools as I learned to use. I couldn't find my feet, to say the least.

So we moved back to Israel with two kids this time, to study Comparative Religion, another less-than-practical course of study. I thought the academic path was about the only path outside the church for those of us interested in religion and spirituality. My wife did not want to be back in Jerusalem. We tried to make the most of it. But after another year and a half, as my school debt grew, staying any longer lost its appeal. And I had a hard time keeping up with all the modern Hebrew I was required to take along with a full course load.

Then, to my surprise, I was offered a job teaching Bible at a Christian high school back home. The war with Lebanon broke out about the same time. I was on the border with Lebanon when it started and could hear the rockets falling all over Galilee from my hotel. So we moved back to Michigan, feeling homeless, but suddenly loving the safety of America and a steady paycheck. The path was winding.

Teaching high school kids was really good for me, probably because my life was not all about me. I needed to calm down a little bit. It was like I had a sort of spiritual PTSD. It felt like I was slowly falling down a hill, from ledge to ledge, deeper into a canyon that I didn't know was there and that seemed to have no bottom. It was as if something started unraveling, and it just kept going and did not stop. The humiliation of the camel bite had given me a good initial shove. I tried very hard to make it stop. I spent time trying to be some Protestant version of Thomas Merton, irregularly keeping the divine hours. I prayed to Saint Francis and the Virgin Mary. *Why Be Catholic?*, by Richard Rohr, sat on the back of the toilet. Then I wanted to be an Orthodox Christian and wondered if I could kiss an icon. I thought that maybe if my faith was as old as possible it would be more genuine and real. I also read the Dalai Lama, Ken Wilber, and Annie Dillard. Show me the way! I quietly groaned.

I couldn't go back to my old beliefs and my old faith, but that's about all I knew. For a long time I was stuck knowing what I wasn't, but not knowing what I was or was becoming. I didn't know how to move forward. There were all kinds of blocks and obstacles in the way, many of which were specific beliefs about God and the spiritual life that no longer rang true. If there was such a thing as a new faith, on the other side of so much unraveling, I had no idea what it looked like. It could not be figured out, just lived through.

I didn't leave Christianity or announce my uncertainties to the world. I just carried them around with me. I think they needed time to work on me. I was the editor of the *NIV First Century Study Bible*, a project I loved that gave me a place to work through all the amazing stuff I'd learned in Israel. Then without warning, Rob Bell stepped down from Mars Hill and a few months later they asked me to apply for his job. I was now a megachurch pastor.

I did a lot of good religious stuff, none of which I regret. In some ways, I did the best I could with the life I was born into. After all, I was raised in the belly of the evangelical church, had the very best religious teachers and models that my tradition could produce. My dad was a pastor, so was my grandpa. My dad was also Jerry Falwell's righthand man when I was kid. I went to Falwell's college. I studied in the Holy Land. I'd been to the top of Sinai and walked where Jesus walked. I worked for one of the fastest-growing churches in America. But it still fell apart.

Most of the falling apart happened in the middle of trying to be religious and in the midst of just living life: raising kids, doing a little self-assessment, and trying to muster the courage to keep going. I was bitten, so to speak, by more than one camel. And after being bitten a few times I started saying more directly, "Wait a minute, this is not working." Certain ideas, theologies, images, and beliefs kept dying, which brought some grief and uncertainty, as well as some anticipation and excitement. Even some of what I thought to be the most important, non-negotiable dimensions of faith no longer seemed necessary.

As a few of the blocks and obstacles cleared, the river of my own spirituality ran more freely, an unexpected gift. But the beliefs and ideas that collapsed were replaced by something more like "hints and guesses," to borrow a line from T. S. Eliot. These hints and guesses were not like the religious certainties I'd grown up with, nor the certainty of some new belief system that I could just exchange for the old one.

Hints and guesses—from my experience, is all we need when our spiritual mountaineering fails to work.

A Short Note to Heresy Hunters

If you're reading this book as a heresy hunter, if you are wondering if I'm a Bible-believing Christian, let me make it easier. I am a heretic and an apostate, and so are my spiritual heroes, like Jesus and Saint Francis. A heretic is one who holds an opinion, which is what the word actually means. I hope one day to hold an opinion, maybe two or three, born out of my own experience of life and of God. And for the record, Jesus wasn't a Bible-believing Christian either. Jesus was killed for holding too many opinions that were dangerously inclusive, unorthodox, and nonbiblical. Jesus was a heretic, before we tamed him and named him Jesus Christ.

If you're wondering if I'm on the slippery slope, let me assure you, I'm at the very bottom. And from this vantage point, way down here, I'm wondering what's next. I'm looking around, and I see a lot of good company. I'm actually not alone. Many others have slid down this slope with me. It's been a pretty wild and exciting ride. We've died a certain kind of death and our ideas have died a certain kind of death. All of which has created some pretty fertile soil. I see new shoots coming up in this soil. I see new life taking root. I see green where I expected to see ash. How did we all end up in this valley, in this blooming desert, in this place of possibility and freedom? It's a gift, a gift of our times, and of a new spirit of existential authenticity and courage.

So, my friends, to those Christians who are deeply uncomfortable with what is happening in the name of Jesus, to those who have doubts, to those teetering on the edge, to those who have left, to those who are spiritually curious: let's find out if there is any food for the soul in the ashes. Let's find out together just how much Christianity and spirituality are evolving. Let's face the reality that our understanding of God is shifting. Let's celebrate the richness of our shared human experience. Let's not play games of worthiness anymore. Let's clear out the blocks to God, even if the word "God" no longer makes sense. Let's clear out the blocks to a fully human, spiritually vibrant, and wildly loving life. Let's embrace the upheaval of our age and trust that the Great Spirit is stirring over the waters of chaos once again. Let's stand on Mount Sinai and embrace the silence of the universe. And let's abandon anything unhelpful.

Let's allow the camel to bite us. In fact, let's stick our arm right in his mouth. Let's touch the teeth marks with our fingers, acknowledging the places we've been wounded but not destroyed. It's not a time for easy explanations or quick fixes. In fact, let's be honest about the places we've been bitten that don't yet make sense. They might just be the things we need to wake us up.

As Saint Francis said on his deathbed:
"Let us begin again,
for up till now
we have done nothing."

2

THE PERILS OF BORDER CROSSING

I used to ride with my friend Matt in his Subaru Justy on the Sabbath from Jerusalem to Bethlehem. Bethlehem had the finest roasted chicken on earth and a homemade garlic sauce that would destroy your breath for days, but it was totally worth it. Most decent restaurants were closed in Jerusalem on the Sabbath, but King David's hometown was open for business. We always had to stop at the makeshift checkpoint the Israeli army had erected on the edge of town. They asked a few benign questions, we showed them our passports, and then they waved us through.

This was during the Second Intifada, the Palestinian uprising, and security kept tightening as the months rolled by. Over time, the Israeli army erected a permanent wall between the West Bank and Israel. Eventually, the wall went right through the neighborhoods between Bethlehem and the outskirts of Jerusalem. Driving from Jerusalem to Bethlehem started taking more time. The checkpoint grew and grew until it was an official border.

Our weekend trips became increasingly difficult, even as Americans with passports. It was obviously much harder for the Palestinians who needed to get back and forth, even if they had all the right papers. But the years of suicide bombings and terrorist attacks had taken their toll and the Israeli government had sealed off the West Bank, as they had done to the Gaza strip.

Then crossing the border changed. We started having to get out of the car so they could search it. They went through our things and checked our bags. I ended up carrying less with me on these trips. It was hardly worth it to take the car anymore. Over time, they added metal detectors and bulletproof glass, railings and queue lines. It felt like we were being stripped of something. In order to get across, we could not carry all we had carried before.

The border crossing ritual started to feel like a metaphor for what was going on in my life. I too was being stripped of my old life, and what I thought I needed seemed less necessary. In fact, the more I carried, the longer the process took. If I was going to be able to cross this metaphoric and spiritual border, I had to leave a bunch of baggage behind. I was going to have to shed just about everything and learn to travel lightly. I started losing bits and pieces of my beliefs, slowly, all while feeling more and more exposed.

My dad worked for Jerry Falwell until I was in junior high. I grew up sitting on Jerry's lap and opening gifts under the Christmas tree from fundamentalist bigwigs. My dad schemed behind closed doors with his friends and dreamed up the Moral Majority, while I played in the woods without a clue that the world was bigger than Lynchburg, Virginia. My mother was raised in the fundamentalist subculture of Bob Jones University. She didn't wear jeans till she was in her late twenties because they weren't holy. She was raised to be a submissive wife, serving the spiritual head of the home and his calling to serve God. And my grandfather was an itinerant Methodist preacher, roaming the country roads of Northern Ireland on his motorcycle. He immigrated to the States to pursue his calling as a pastor. Faith ran in the family.

So walking away, even slowly, from any of my beliefs required shedding the only clothes I'd ever known. It was unclear to me if I would freeze or if I really didn't need all the extra layers.

It came in fits and starts, with second-guesses and an occasional retreat back to safer ground. Sometimes I wondered if I would go back to being a Bible-believing Christian, get over all my doubts, and return to the faith. I could hear the voices of my childhood accusing me of "backsliding" and calling for my repentance. I could hear Falwell's warning about the dangers of becoming "secular." And it was scary. I didn't want to disappoint people. But I couldn't stay loyal to some version of faith that wasn't mine anymore. It turns out, by some grace, I had been dragged, kicking and screaming and cursing and doubting, to a border between one land and another.

Loyal Soldiers and Good Failures

I sat one morning in an elders' meeting at church, fiddling with my fruit plate. One elder was talking about how hard it was to defend her involvement at Mars Hill to her family. Rob Bell had left a big wake with his teachings and books. She looked at me, the new pastor, and said, "I just don't want to have to explain Mars Hill anymore at the Thanksgiving table. I hope you're not planning anything controversial this year. We're all tired of controversy."

Part of me understood where she was coming from. Trying to explain your politics or religious convictions at the Thanksgiving table is a nightmare for almost anyone. But another part of me wanted to give an impassioned plea for justice and truth, saying that Jesus had been killed for being controversial. If we were serious about Jesus, we would be controversial to someone, somewhere. But in the end, I said nothing, or nothing important. All of a sudden, being true to myself felt unsafe. And in that moment, I wondered who I was and what I was doing there. I left feeling like a fraud. I could either keep hiding in a room full of people, or I could own what I needed to own.

There were questions bouncing around in my head. Who do I need to please? Who do I need to be loyal to? How can I survive here without too much damage? These voices were more unconscious than explicit. I guess I was trying to be a good boy for the church people (though the definitions of being good kept shifting depending on whom I was talking to).

I came to understand that these voices were the inner Loyal Soldier. I learned about this from Richard Rohr, and later from Bill Plotkin. The image comes from World War II.[1] A few Japanese soldiers were stranded on islands in the South Pacific years after the war was over, but they didn't know the war was over. Their commitment and loyalty to the war is what kept them alive—it was their survival strategy. They couldn't have made it through their suffering without a loyal commitment to the war. So it is with our childhood survival strategies. We couldn't have survived the traumas and hardships of childhood without them. They kept us alive. But they continue to function, even years after the war of childhood is over.

My own Loyal Soldier kept me safe enough. I learned the language, the actions, the behaviors, the rituals, the outfits, and the beliefs to be socially accepted in American evangelicalism. But at a certain point, the Loyal Soldier's job is over. I really didn't need this voice to remain safe and accepted in my twenties or thirties. It was time to move on, to thank the soldier for all his work, and relieve him of his duties.

When we get to the border of something unknown—like when we face our disbelief, or question what we've been told about God—our Loyal Soldier often gets called into service. Whatever strategies kept us safe growing up is all the Loyal Soldier knows. His voice can be so loud that we never really get going. Instead, we back

---

1. Check out the writings and programs of Bill Plotkin. See *Soulcraft: Crossing into the Mysteries of Nature and Psyche* (Novato, CA: New World Library, 2003), 91–96. See also Richard Rohr, *Falling Upward* (San Francisco: Jossey-Bass, 2011), 44.

away. This is okay from time to time, and nothing to be ashamed about. But remaining loyal to what's safe and comfortable doesn't help us grow up.

A few of us get lucky in this struggle for a more authentic sense of self. We fail, despite the advice of the soldier, which pushes us further across the border. We get divorced. Our kid leaves home. We get fired. We commit some public sin. We stop believing. We get the corner office and still feel empty. We buy the dream car and are looking on Craigslist the next day for a better one. We graduate from seminary, with all the right answers, and feel like we haven't even started a real relationship with God. Raising kids turns out to be really hard. Our spouse cheats on us. We cheat, and get caught. The leadership in our church fails us. The Christian school we paid for doesn't keep our kids morally or spiritually safe. We get sick. Our daughter announces she is gay. Our dad comes out of the closet. Our partner wants an open relationship. We have a captive and gracious megachurch audience of thousands of people and we no longer know what to say. Life doesn't go as planned, even though we tried.

But these failures are gifts that open the door just a crack. At this point, the Loyal Soldier goes into overdrive. He screams. She shames. The Loyal Soldier tries to keep us safe by telling us not to go any further. Best to retry all the same programs that gave us a sense of identity in the first place. Go back to church. Join a small group. Really commit to pray this time. Memorize the Bible. Listen to Christian Radio. Give tithes and offerings to the church. Any technique that will protect us from vulnerability and the truth of our own life will do. The Loyal Soldier would be perfectly happy if we would remain the same and pretend like nothing's happening.

But the Loyal Soldier can't save us. His battle plans are for old battles; they're out-of-date, and his ammunition is worthless. Life's not working and neither are the old survival strategies. This is what happened to me; I could not go further and still attempt to please the old voices in my head.

OUT-OF-BODY SUNDAY

One morning I walked around the portable stage at Mars Hill giving a sermon. I could feel it swaying a bit under my feet. The church had grown so fast, so soon, that in the early days we gave no thought to permanent stages or even basic safety concerns. The stage was in the center of the room, so there was no good place to hide. I had my notes on a black music stand. Thousands of faces were looking at me. And I loved teaching, so part of me felt right at home. But on this Sunday, I was totally unprepared for what happened.

Suddenly I could see myself teaching from above. It was like I slipped out of my own skin. I watched myself walking around the stage. I could hear words coming out of my mouth, but I thought, "Who is that speaking? What is he talking about?" Somehow I kept going. I forced myself to just keep talking. Part of me was calm, almost disengaged, wondering "Who is that on stage?" But I also felt a tremor of panic watching myself, knowing that I didn't believe what

I was saying. This lasted until my sermon was over, which felt like a lifetime. I walked off the stage and tried to get out of the building as fast as possible. At first, I vowed to never speak again till I figured out what was happening. I didn't keep the vow, but I couldn't shake the feeling that came over me. Was I going insane?

Something had split. One part of me was doing what it always did, and doing it really well. He knew the right words; he knew a few funny jokes and clever asides. He was used to walking around saying things. But there was also a *me* that was not the me giving the sermon. So I started asking questions about this out-of-body thing that happened. I started wondering, in a more serious way, "Who am I?"

I feared there was no answer to this question—nothing down there, deep inside, no true self, no deeper self, only a great nothingness. This fear of annihilation, of being nobody, is another part of my own loyal soldier work. All the people of authority in my life worked in very public ministries of one sort or another. To perform was to be seen and loved and accepted. But the subconscious is more powerful than I knew. Feeding a public self-image was merely a strategy for avoiding being nobody.

Eventually, something—looking back, I think it was grace, or love—kept piercing parts my persona, or ego, or whatever you want to call it. It deflated a little. And I started venturing near the black hole of being nobody, only to discover there was a *me* who was in there somewhere. One day I realized that I was pursuing a kind of social acceptance at the cost of personal authenticity. It's not that I knew exactly what being authentic was. I just knew I could not find out if I continued the roles I had grown accustomed to. Like Jesus said, "What if you gain the whole world and forfeit your soul?" I had gained so much. I was grateful for the good church people in my life, and the decent living I made, but at what cost to my inner life? I started getting really curious about discovering the deeper self, or the soul, or the *me* underneath the roles I played.

But be warned, the Loyal Soldier doesn't give up his post easily. He's saving me from certain death, that's his firm belief. In a way, when I was kid, he did save me. I grew up in a fundamentalist culture that taught me that if I didn't believe the right things and obey the right rules, not only would I die and be separated from everyone and everything that I loved, but I would be tortured in hell for all eternity. We even had a hierarchy of vocations that God approved of. At the very top was pastor; a close second was missionary. In these roles, I could be the safest and most respected. And that worked for a long time. Until it didn't. And then it *really* didn't.

The vocation of preaching requires the occasional bending of the truth. Sometimes we've got to preach faith even when we're struggling with doubt. Every pastor and rabbi and imam and priest knows what I'm talking about. There's an invisible line we also know is there, "This far you shall come, but no further." This is probably why Jesus never worked for an organized religion. The pull to keep the group intact is often stronger than the pull of the truth.

I had to be honest that my own wheels had come off.

And I had to be honest that I believed the wheels needed to come off. So I quit.

GO FORTH

Abram had to leave his country, his people, and his father's household. He had to leave every identity marker in his life. There would be no story if Abram did not leave. His name would've never grown into Abraham. He would've never met the Mystery that beckoned him in the first place. His path wasn't simple or clear. He didn't even know to what country he was being called. It was dark, and he didn't know what he was doing; he doubted, he also believed, and when he died he did not know if his two sons were going to kill each other or if they would really be the fathers of two great nations. Not even Abraham could see the whole picture.

I had to try all kinds of things. I had to move to Israel. I had to check out Judaism for a while. I had to climb Sinai. I had to get really lost. I had to teach. I had to try on being a scholar. I had to work for the church. I had to be the spiritual-answer-man. I had to climb the ladder of spiritual success.

But there was a voice that kept quietly saying, "Leave." Sometimes it was just a sensation in my body. No matter, the call was real. It felt like being drawn out beyond the confines of what I'd known. To take any risk at all, to leave home even a little bit, is just the beginning. It's the beginning of admitting we're looking for something that pre-packaged religion, with its glut of answers and certitudes, just isn't delivering.

Personally, I was looking for God. I was looking for a more authentic spirituality. I was looking for meaning and for a place to call home. I was searching for convictions and ideas that resonated with my own experience, and for a few new experiences. I tried to make sense of my evangelical past along the way. At times I ran full speed away from my past, and at others times I ran toward it.

But at first I didn't find what I was looking for, and this is a sign that I had merely started to cross the border. Being bitten by a camel is exactly the pattern of real invitation. Had I received the answers to all my prayers, been given golden tablets of divine instruction or a readymade job description, the story couldn't be trusted—stories where people find exactly what they're looking for can rarely be trusted. Because I felt like a spiritual failure, I had accidently stumbled onto the fertile ground of real change.

I meet people all the time who feel like spiritual failures. This is great news! It means we've started another journey, we're on a larger quest, we're going forth like Abram. I want to stand up and cheer, "Go for it!"

The Bible is full of failures. Moses, a murderer, was running from his past and from his God when he accidently stumbled onto holy ground. Jonah was fleeing his destiny when God suddenly swallowed him up. Jacob was escaping from his brother after cheating him out of money when he had a most disturbing dream. The woman caught in adultery, about to be stoned to death by religious authorities, happens to be dragged first before a peasant-preacher named Jesus. The profound path starts when things don't work out. Jesus's family, friends, and closest disciples rejected him. Only then did the real path of going down become painfully clear as the real path of change. The Hollywood path of conquest is the opposite of real transformation. Nothing is learned when we win all the time.

Listen to Joseph Campbell on the matter: "We have only to follow the thread of the hero path. Where we had thought to find an abomination, we shall find a god; where we had thought to slay another, we shall slay ourselves; where we had thought to travel outwards, we shall come to the center of our existence; where we had thought to be alone, we shall be with all the world."[2]

Whatever we're seeking comes as a total surprise. It's not what we thought. And it's only a thread. Reality doesn't work the way we imagined. We go out seeking victory and are defeated. If we're lucky, we go into the earth, under the water, into the abyss, into the tomb, into the womb again, into the cocoon. Here is where the mystery of transformation takes place. The caterpillar seems to be dying, and in a way it is. If it doesn't go toward its own death, it will never fly as a new creation.

I went out to find God, and God wasn't there. Everything I ever learned about God fell apart. Turns out this had to happen for me to grow up. And in my view, a lot of our theology, our images of God, our doctrines, our beliefs,

---

2. Joseph Campbell, *The Hero with a Thousand Faces* (Princeton, NJ: Princeton University Press, 1973).

have to fall apart for us to keep going. The ashes become the fruitful ground for new growth. Let our kids reject the whole lot. Let our church be unable to pay the bills. Let our spouse be honest about his or her real experience. Let's go out with our neighbors and ask them questions about meaning, and God, and life, and don't pretend we know the truth anymore. There's nothing to fear.

THE EYE OF THE NEEDLE

In the ancient city of Megiddo there is a very narrow gate that zigzags its way to a small entrance. You can hop the fence if no park rangers are near and walk on the ancient steps. Most likely, this gate was used at night, or when it was too dangerous to open the main city gate. Legend has it this kind of gate was called the "eye of the needle." In order for the camels, the semi-trucks of the desert, to pass through the gate they had to be stripped of all their baggage.

Jesus said to his followers, "It is easier for a camel to pass through the eye of a needle than for a rich man to enter the kingdom of heaven." This is a story about all of us, a border-crossing kind of story. No wonder I was attacked by a camel. The camel was the very image of so much of what needed to be stripped from my own life.

We tend to think that faith is about loading up the camel for the long haul, but it's just the opposite. All our certainties about God and the truth have turned us into the rich man in Jesus's story. To cross the border, to pass through the gate, a lot of stuff needs to be unloaded. For me, my beliefs about original sin, the afterlife, the Bible, end times, salvation, knowledge of God, and an extra-special spiritual life all had come off the back of the camel. As Jesus says, it's the only path to the kingdom. We all must be laid bare.

My prayer is that we will set a few burdens down and heed the call to go forth. My hope is that we will cross the border, even though there are voices screaming at us to stop. We will have to leave a few cherished things behind and travel lightly. But it's a gentle invitation, not a demand. We can say "no." But it's a call that promises new life on the other side of our impending spiritual death. A new kingdom awaits. It's a call where new "hints and guesses" about what is ultimately true and real emerge in the desert we thought would be barren. So let's leave home, cross the border, go through the eye of the needle and see what happens.

3

YOU ARE NOT A PROBLEM TO GOD

I flew to Spain when I was fifteen with dozens of other teenagers on a mission trip. We went to tell the Spaniards about Jesus because we thought Catholics were not saved. We sang Christian rap songs in Spanish (which few of us spoke), did choreographed gymnastics, and generally made asses of ourselves in public squares wearing MC Hammer pants, already a few years out of style. At the end of each performance, we told the dumbstruck crowd how to get saved and go to heaven when they died. We counted the number of salvations by a show of hands, which justified our mission to the parents and grandparents who put up the money for our adventure.

On the flight over, I sat with my childhood friend Jon. We hadn't seen each other in a few years, and we were both full of hormones and wild ideas. I stole a beer from the drink cart as it passed by. We downed the Cokes we had been drinking and then carefully split the beer by pouring it into the empty soda cans. It was more of a joke than anything, but one I failed to hide from the girls who sat behind us.

After a few days the rumors started up. "Jon and Kent got drunk on the plane." Sure, we acted like drunken idiots, but we always did. The truth was, we were also smoking in our hotel bathroom, sneaking girls into our room at night, and doing all manner of mischievous things. We were teenagers on an overseas trip. A few of our friends had actually gone to the bar, so we weren't the only ones breaking rules.

It's worth noting that Jon and I were both pastors' kids, making us likely targets for blame. Any chance to point out our errors was done with smugness: "I would expect nothing less from you. You know better. What sinners!"

As soon as the rumors started swirling, I went into full denial mode. I worked so hard at this elaborate game that I finally won over a few adults. I convinced one leader not only to believe me, but to be my public defender. I played the victim card, that no one ever believes me because I'm the pastor's kid, it's so unfair, etc. He was eating out of my hand, poor guy. But everything spun out of control. Students were called in one at a time to see the director. The adults gathered evidence. They threatened to send home anyone who sinned.

This went on for several days before I finally broke. The director came to me, made an apology, and asked for *my* forgiveness. He said he understood how I must feel, with all these unfair rumors and lies about me. He knew I was good kid. He was sorry. Then I told him it was actually true. He was stunned. Jon and I were pulled from the outdoor witnessing gymnastics carnival, and we waited for our punishments.

It was too expensive to fly us home. Instead, they decided that we'd be confined to the missionary's house on the top floor of a huge apartment complex in Barcelona for the rest of the week. (Turns out this was my first taste of real Spain. The missionary kids went out to bring us bread and cheese from the market. I had never tasted something so simple and so amazing.) We spent the days watching crowds passing from the balcony. But before all that, we were summoned to a group meeting. We had to confess our sins before the students, the chaperones, the parents, the missionaries, and the other churches we were working with.

We gathered in the park before another one of our shows. Jon and I were brought up on stage. A verse was read: "If we confess our sins, he is faithful to forgive us our sins and cleanse us from all unrighteousness." The director talked about the sinners who were on the trip and their sins that had nearly ruined our testimony to the Spaniards. The director handed me the microphone and asked me if I had anything to say. Everyone was staring. I started crying. I hated myself for crying. I was crying out of embarrassment more than remorse. Jon held it together in his confession. But I had lost all the coolness that I was trying so hard to exude. I finally got the words out, "I'm sorry. I drank part of a beer on the plane."

I could see a friend sitting a few feet away who had gone to the bar. He sat calmly, without the slightest intention of admitting his guilt. He had a fake-earnest look of concern on his face. The director asked for other confessions. No one came forward. Jon and I just stood there in the giant spotlight of public shame. He explained our punishment, then he prayed. I can't remember exactly what he said, but there was a lot of asking God to forgive our wickedness and to protect our testimony here in Spain. He basically blamed any failure to evangelize the Spanish on one can of beer.

BORN IN "SIN"

I didn't recover quickly from this humiliation. When I got back home I was kicked off the church's water ski team. (Yes, we actually had such a thing. We gave the good news about Jesus after barefooting and doing human pyramids.) But the embarrassment I felt was deeper than just getting in trouble. It was just the kind of thing I had so often experienced in my tradition: a lot of shame, a lot of pain, and a lot of finger-pointing.

I was a problem to God, and to everyone else. Ever since I was a kid, the unequivocal starting place was that I am a sinner. In fact, step one in becoming a Christian was admitting I was in the wrong. My sin was not just a matter of poor choices or mistakes. I was born this way. From the moment of my first breath, I was a problem to God. I inherited this problem from Adam and Eve. I was told, and I also believed, despite all evidence to the contrary, that my "heart was desperately wicked."

The God I believed in couldn't stand any sin. This

meant God couldn't stand the way I was born. What's more, he was unable to even look at me. He couldn't even look at his own son on the cross because Jesus was carrying all my sins. My sins—beer and cigarettes and lies and girls—had crucified Jesus. I imagined him hanging there with all my mischievous deeds on his back. I was taught that if I were the only person on earth, Jesus would still have to be tortured to death—my sin was that bad. My true nature deserved eternal torture in the flames of hell. My sin was so ugly that it could only be covered by Jesus's blood—but only if I really believed in this bloody atonement and never doubted.

This was totally paralyzing. Every day I feared that I hadn't said the right prayer or hadn't meant it enough. Every day I was afraid the blood of Jesus didn't cover my sin. From my earliest memories until I was in my teens. I asked Jesus to save me from my sins at least once per week, I was taught that if I was truly saved, then I wouldn't sin anymore, or only rarely. The problem was that I kept sinning, therefore I must not be truly saved. This is a vicious cycle of guilt, shame, and fear.

Thomas Road Baptist Church, which Jerry Falwell pastored, put on an Easter pageant every year when I was kid. The highlight was the hanging of a college kid with a spray tan from a massive wooden cross. We sat mesmerized by the fog machine and the sounds of the iron spikes being driven through his hands. The message was always the same: we were born in sin and we had caused Jesus to suffer like this. If we didn't get right with God, we would end up being tortured like this forever. I look back at these messages twenty-five years later in amazement. It is a miracle any of us survived.

These are not benign messages. This is a kind of child abuse, and I'm not being flippant. The church I grew up in did tremendous damage to young people by telling them they're a problem to God from their first breath. The church wounded people with its low view of human beings and its narrow view of God. The message is about our fundamental essence. According to this worldview, our true essence is both sinful and unworthy of God. And once you've been initiated into this way of thinking, it's hard to shake.

Many of the conversations I had as a pastor were related to these central messages, because many faithful people in the church have never had their own goodness reflected back to them. Behind their questions is a simple longing to know, "Am I okay?" Sadly, much of Christianity says, "No. You're not okay. But if you do exactly what we say, or believe exactly the right things, God will overlook your deep unworthiness. And keep coming to church, so we can keep telling you how to do it, because you're probably doing it wrong. Don't forget how evil your true nature really is."

When my first daughter Lucy was born, I came face-to-face with such a beautiful person, such a plump being of light, that whatever I'd been told about the nature of being human had to be false. It was almost terrifying to fall in love so immediately and so wholeheartedly, to feel so responsible and so helpless at the same time. But to believe my daughter was a problem to God was unthinkable. Her essence wasn't sinful. Her essence was mystery and goodness. She did not need to be covered by blood. She didn't need a special prayer or magical baptismal water to be accepted by God. I loved my daughter just the way she was, and I was sure that God did, too. I didn't need anything more from her, or wish she were born with a better essence. And this is merely human love. It cannot be true that God is less loving than I am.

As she grew up, once or twice I heard from my parents about her "sinful nature" when she did normal toddler things, like throw herself on the ground in protest. Apparently, if Adam and Eve hadn't sinned and screwed everything up, parenting would be much easier. I remember hearing as a kid that Jesus never cried, because he was sinless—we even sing about it at Christmas: "But little Lord Jesus, no crying he makes." So crying was another sin. I used to think about him completely silent in his manger, the ultimate good boy for Mary and Joseph. This is completely absurd. Not to mention, later in life, the Bible says clearly enough that "Jesus wept." What a relief.

Religious shame, fear, and its depraved view of human beings are serious problems, problems that go way back. Not all the way to Adam and Eve, but to the early days of Christianity.

THE FALLACY OF ORIGINAL SIN

There's a Christian doctrine called "original sin." It's predicated on a creator who cannot celebrate his own creation's essence, just as it is, mistakes and messiness, beauty and loveliness. This God is a moral policeman in the sky, a tyrannical parent. If you saw parents in the grocery store who were demanding perfection from their kids, you'd probably consider calling the authorities, yet we somehow think God is a perfection tyrant.

We have to start from a better place. When you get the beginning of the story wrong, the whole thing grows into a monster. We cannot start with shame and with such a low view of human beings. We cannot start with, "You are a problem to God." We cannot tell people they are totally unworthy. So we cannot start with "original sin." We cannot tell people they deserve hell by virtue of just being alive. There is no good news to be found in that story.

Plus, we can't say that our hyper-focus on sin has served us very well. There's so much addiction, scandal, and abuse in the church I grew up in. It's a cliché that the pastor's kid is a drug addict and a delinquent, but it's an image I lived into quite well. It's a cliché that fundamentalist kids go off the rails, which happened to a lot of my friends. We aren't surprised when the pastor sleeps with the secretary, which happened to more than one of my dad's closest associates. When you believe that your core identity is a problem, you end up fulfilling this negative image. The constant use of shame and rules only makes the situation more intolerable. You can even use original sin to justify bad behavior: "I guess I really am a wretched sinner. That's why I did this. I'm pretty much worthless. Forgive me, I'll try harder next time." And the cycle continues.

Many of us believe that wretchedness is our true identity. This is one of the biggest problems in the church today, particularly the church I grew up in. But the church's messages about human worth have also influenced Western culture, so it's not just a problem in the pews.

Let me confess something as a former pastor: it's the easiest thing in the world to preach a shaming message. I admit, it slipped into my own sermons. I am sorry. It's so easy to put others down, giving them the subtle message they're a problem to God. This actually pays the bills. A lot of churches make a living on this kind of shame, for it creates a strange co-dependency.

When I first started to see this, all of a sudden I saw it everywhere. It was in the children's curriculum, in the sermon, in our programs, in our books, in our music. One Sunday I made a commitment that I would never again say anything that reinforced the foundationally negative starting place of original sin, total depravity, or atonement theology. I discovered that it was easier said than done. After a chat with my worship leader, we agreed to try to avoid songs that reinforce these messages. Ninety percent of the worship songs and hymns were suddenly off limits.

The roots of original sin go back to the church fathers. It's not in the Bible. In the fourth century, Augustine, the larger-than-life church father whose writings so deeply changed Christianity, argued that sin was passed on like eye color or physical traits. It wasn't matter of poor human choices. Original sin, he said, came from your father's semen. (This by the way, is one reason why sex got such a bad reputation in the church. Making babies was the same as making more sinners, so the act itself must also be sinful.)

To be human, in other words, was to be in deep trouble with God from the beginning—the moment of conception.

Augustine had a lot of regrets from his life of wild partying before he became a Christian. Like we all do, he was trying to work through his own issues. His *Confessions* are haunting and beautiful. But his view on personhood has got to go. He is not even the sole voice on the matter. The entire Eastern half of Christianity never accepted original sin in the first place, so there's no need to think it came down from Sinai or the Sermon on the Mount. "Original sin" was just one interpretation on being a human being. But we should no longer start in such a depraved place.

Original sin is done, it's over.

THE QUESTION OF SIN

Original sin is miles from what the Bible originally meant by sin in the first place. You may have heard that the word for sin in Hebrew means to "miss the mark." We're all on the path, or moving along the sacred way of life, by virtue of the fact that we are alive. And we are also prone to miss the target from time to time. When we sin, we fail to live our best lives. We are hurt, as much as we hurt the world around us. When people live in destructive ways, the entire community suffers.

The specific sins in the Bible were expressions of the ancient culture in which the Bible was written. Abstaining from pork, or not cutting the side of your hair, these were human ways of trying to differentiate from the neighboring cultures. These laws helped keep the community's identity intact. In my view, to call them direct laws from God is to miss the point. They were interpretive laws, based on Israel's own cultural experiences and their evolving understanding of God. Yet other laws in the Bible transcend their cultural starting place. To take care of the widow and the orphan, to refrain from a life of envy, to love your neighbor, are all flashes of insight that still shine light on the path we walk.

Sin is more like a question: What are ways of living that cause suffering? What are ways of living that disintegrate our God-given wholeness? The question of what it means to miss the mark is a metaphor worth thinking about. Right now, our modern way of life is causing all kinds of suffering. We're missing the mark in all kinds of ways. In this sense, human beings "sin."

But many of the sins of the Bible are no longer sins. And most people know this anyway; they just don't know it's okay to admit it. Men can have long hair. Women can speak in church. These aren't permitted in the Bible, but our understanding of God is always evolving. The first Christians stopped circumcising their children as a requirement to be in the family of God. Hurray! They defied one law because they were listening to another law, the one forming in their hearts.

Jesus never said to stop circumcision or eat a BLT. But the community founded in his name went on to wrestle with these things in their own way. Jesus even gave away this kind of power when he said that the Spirit "will guide you into truth." The shifts in the early church around sin, law, and divine acceptance took courage and sounded like heresy at first. But thank God they had the courage to challenge the status quo, and even to challenge their understanding of God. Our cultural ways of living in harmony with one another, with nature, and with God, will always be evolving.

Very slowly, I started to imagine God as something other than a rule enforcer. This image started to give way. I began to look to justice, love of neighbor, and mercy as my deeper guides, as they were for the prophets and for Jesus. These are not laws exactly. They're images of goodness. Following God was never about keeping the rules—just read the prophets if you don't believe me. The sins in the Bible simply reveal patterns of human behavior that are destructive. The patterns matter more than the specifics.

In other words, there is a great dance between personal freedom, responsibility, communal needs, the wisdom of the past, and the Spirit of God. We're still dancing. And don't worry so much about getting it wrong. We all get something wrong. Big deal, you're not going to burn in hell.

All this is to say, people miss the mark. But they're not originally sinful.

ORIGINAL GOODNESS

My wife came up from the basement one day and asked, "What if I'm not a problem to God? What if there is no problem?"

It caught me off guard, such a straightforward question. The truth was, I didn't believe it anymore. I just didn't know I didn't believe it. Her questions pulled a few more beliefs off the back of the camel.

This is really important work that often happens on the threshold on the border. All of a sudden, we recognize that our espoused theology and our practical theology are no longer in alignment. We discover that our adopted theology and our living theology are out of whack. This is a chance to wake up, to get curious about this lack of alignment. When people sat in my church office sharing their hearts, many of their struggles were rooted in this lack of alignment. This was the same lack of alignment I felt on the top of Sinai but didn't have words for at the time.

I am not a problem to God. Neither is my wife. Or anyone.

God doesn't have to fix me in order to accept me. I've got problems for sure, but my essence is not a problem to God.

I am originally good. We all are.

And what we need, more than anything else, is for our own goodness to be reflected back to us. This ought to be the full-time job of the church or any spiritual community. We're already *good,* in the deepest recesses of our being. And contact with this original *goodness* is needed to heal all the broken and fragmented parts of our lives, the problems we have created, and the ones that just happened to us, by no fault of our own. Embracing our original goodness is absolutely essential.

After I got back from Israel, my wife and I took a year-long class from the Dominican Sisters on spiritual formation. They encouraged us to find a spiritual director to help us talk about where we were in our spiritual lives. The title "spiritual director" is a bit misleading—they're more like deep listeners. They reflect back to you your own goodness and what they hear you saying. They listen with the ears of their hearts, so to speak. They help you draw out those hidden springs of real desire and longing. They create a safe space for the true self to come out of hiding. It's a holy and beautiful thing.

When I first sat with a spiritual director, I thought I might come unglued. I was in despair. I spilled my doubts and anger about the church, my parents, and Jerusalem. I complained about being in the wrong denomination and the wrong religion. I told this lovely nun that I didn't feel like I was a Christian anymore. As my tears flowed, she just smiled at me. Then she said, "Calm down. What you are going through is normal. You're okay. Everything in the spiritual life takes time and happens slowly. You're a good person, and you're lucky to have such diverse experiences."

Lucky? Good? Stay calm? This wasn't what I expected to hear. I thought I might hear the same messages of guilt mixed with a little advice to just try harder. But it turned out that I really needed my own original goodness reflected back to me. And she was doing just that. I needed to hear that it was going to be okay. I needed to hear that I was already okay. Without a good mirror reminding us we are okay, it's very hard to go further on the path of transformation. My relationships with the two spiritual directors I've had are two of the most important mirrors in my life.

Experiences of our deep goodness are true spiritual experiences. I've had a few of them. They tend to come out of blue, like sitting in an office with a nun. Or sometimes when I'm not thinking at all about my spiritual life. I had one such experience on the way home from class in Jerusalem. I was lying on the grass, watching families in the park, watching the light change on the olives tress. The season of Lent had me thinking about repentance. Earlier in the day I wrote an angry outburst about my fundamentalist upbringing on a tiny scrap of paper. After spewing all kinds of venom, I looked down at the paper and smiled. I thought, "Really, that's it." A lightness in my body took over. Yes, I was angry and hurt, but in getting it out, it seemed to lose its sting. "So what?" I thought. It seemed to have lost its power over me.

I took out the piece of paper, wadded it up, and shoved it into a sewer pipe a few feet away. I had no profound religious thoughts or questions. A calm feeling came over me where all my religious doubts and yearnings, all my failures and heartache, seemed okay. Up until that moment, everything in Jerusalem was a huge theological problem to be solved. I didn't solve any problems in that moment—I just experienced goodness and grace in the afternoon light. I didn't need to be covered by Jesus's blood. I didn't need to be covered by anything. In fact, the real me was just starting to come out of hiding. And I felt loved. It didn't last all that long, but my original goodness shined through for a moment and I could see the same goodness all around me in the park. You don't have to call this an encounter with God or a spiritual experience, but that's what I call it.

Amnesia set in moments later. Amnesia is why we need spiritual directors, real friends, and spiritual voices that tell us to pay attention to our own lives, our own experiences, and to trust that God is in the middle of them.

LOVING YOURSELF

I was leading a tour to Israel a few years ago with a group of students and adults. I was at a place called Gamla, a city known for its resistance against the Romans in the Great Jewish Revolt. I gave what I thought to be a rousing teaching on Zealot ideology and Jesus's radical claim to love your enemies instead of resisting them. I was making a big deal out of the commandment, "Love your neighbor as yourself." Then one of the college students spoke up. She asked, "What if you don't love yourself?"

There have only been a few times in my teaching career that I've been stopped in my tracks, and this was one of them. I really didn't know what to say, other than, "Good point," followed by, "I don't know, no one has ever asked me that." So we just sat around for a while and talked about how important her question was, even without knowing the answer.

Her words haunted me for months. How can we love someone else when our own self-image has been beaten down by both religion and our celebrity culture? Love-of-self is mocked in religious circles as being selfish, new agey, and unholy. The image most of us have of ourselves is not worth loving. The image many of us have is one of utter depravity and unworthiness. We hope to be loved by someone else, if we're lucky, because we cannot accept ourselves. This is a heavy burden.

Human beings, no matter their gender, ethnicity, sexual orientation, or zip code, are all created in the image of God and called "very good." This is the opening image of humanity in the Bible. This image is our divine DNA, our original goodness. We cannot screw it up or do anything to lose it. It is the face we had before we were born, to borrow a Buddhist saying. Each of us reflects the divine DNA in our own complicated and beautiful way. And this ought to be the church's primary message. It's right in the heart of the Christian tradition, it's just been drowned out. "When you see your brother or sister, you see God," says the second-century theologian Clement of Alexandria. No amount of sin can mess up this divine DNA. This is real gospel.

This is one of the points of the Garden of Eden story. It's a reminder of what's down there, deeply, in the recesses of our soul and psyche, a garden of union with nature and with God. That is, a garden of communion and belonging.

I'm not saying we're perfect, I'm saying perfection is not the point. We're originally good and also a little messy. This is a more honest way of naming our moral ambiguity. Even in our muddled mess, there is a truth greater than our sins, failures, and mistakes.

The image of Jesus invites us to descend. We die, as he died, to our fragmented self and the stories we have believed, especially stories of unworthiness. We descend, only to find we are already home. Something purely good is at the seat of our being. We actually lose ourselves, only to find our true selves. We are not covered up. We are uncovered. Our nakedness becomes our acceptance, just like Jesus's naked acceptance of his enemies on the cross.

Listen to Thomas Merton:

> *In the center of our being is a point of nothingness which is untouched by sin and by illusion, a point of pure truth, a point or spark which belongs entirely to God, which is never at our disposal, from which God disposes our lives, which is inaccessible to the fantasies of our own mind or the brutalities of our own will. This little point of nothingness and of absolute poverty is the pure glory of God in us.*
>
> *It is like a pure diamond, blazing with the invisible light of heaven. It is in everybody, and if we could see it we would see these billions of points of light coming together in the face and blaze of the sun that would make all the darkness and cruelty of life vanish completely. I have no program for this seeing. It is only given. But the gate of heaven is everywhere.*[1]

---

1. Thomas Merton, *Conjectures of a Guilty Bystander* (New York: Image Books/ Doubleday Religion, 2009), 155.

This is such good news that I could cry. We belong. We matter. We are loved. Love created us and we're going to be okay. We're already okay. Every aspect of our true selves belongs in the world and is the goodness of the world coming into being. We're an expression of God, born into the world in this moment, an incarnation, a divine breath. Not less than human, but fully human.

As a few of the unhelpful beliefs about original sin were unloaded, the burden lightened in my own spiritual life. And in the spaces left, something more beautiful began to take its place. The hint and guess is that we are far more beautiful to God, just as we are, than I ever imagined.

4

WORRY ABOUT THE AFTERLIFE, AFTER LIFE

One hot afternoon in Jerusalem, I was walking home with the rabbi who taught my Rabbinic Judaism class. We turned north from Mount Zion, down into the Hinnom Valley where there is little shade. I picked a few stems of rosemary from the hundreds of bushes in the valley, breathing in the scent as we strolled along. Passing from shade to sun in the dry air, nearly 3,000 feet above sea level, had become familiar on these afternoon walks.

We chatted about the afterlife, *Gehennah*, hell, and the differences between the Catholic and Jewish prayers for the dead. It sounds like a heavy conversation, but the rabbi was full of lightness and humor. He seemed amused by my seriousness. I'd been working on a paper for his class about the various perspectives on the afterlife from the first and second centuries. He carried hundreds of references on the shelves of his mind and I was eager for him to divulge as much as possible.

Then, I was overcome with the urge to ask him the most important question of my entire religious upbringing: "If you were to die right now, are you absolutely sure you would go to heaven?"

This was the only question that really mattered to my tribe of Christians, the question beyond all questions. It explained all our heartfelt devotion and churchgoing. The point of believing in Jesus was eternal life in heaven. It was that simple: no Jesus, no heaven.

I blurted out the question, then I felt a hot flash of embarrassment. I forgot any sort of setup. I gave him no warning. It sounded like I was witnessing to him, evangelizing the rabbi. He paused for moment, looking at me. I thought maybe he didn't hear me. I stumbled over the question, again.

He smiled and said softly, "That's not an important question."

He started to walk again, like that settled that. It was clear he had nothing more to say on the matter. I protested, "Yes, it *is* an important question. Just about every church service I ever went to growing up ended with this question." I took a few quick steps to come alongside him again. "It's at the heart of why most of us believe in Jesus."

He said, "It's not an important question to me, or to Judaism."

His words kept rolling over in my head. I was stunned. Such a simple response that sounded so true. *Not an impor-*

tant question. And I wanted so badly for this to be the case. The obsession with the afterlife felt like one more layer that needed shedding for me to go any further.

People can say all they want that Christianity isn't really about going to heaven, but let's be honest, for many Christians that's exactly what it's about. I, however, no longer wanted to live as if my real life was coming later, after I die. I no longer wanted to argue about someone's eternal address. I wanted it not to be an important question for me, either.

WHAT *IS* IMPORTANT . . . TO JESUS

Jesus does not talk about how to go to heaven in the Gospels. He never tells people that life is about going somewhere when we die. He mentions a future reality only a few times. Once he tells a story about the final judgment, the separation of the sheep and goats, but the imperative is to live now as if every hungry, thirsty, sick, and imprisoned person is to be loved and cared for, right now. Another time he mentions preparing rooms in his father's house. This could be a reference to heaven, but the temple in Jerusalem was also called God's house, so we cannot be so certain. Then he leads his disciples up to the temple in Jerusalem and makes a big scene about how *this* house should be a place of prayer for all nations. He's targeted, tracked down, and arrested because of this public act of enfolding all people into the kingdom of God's family in the here and now. And anyway, Jesus was a first-century Jew, shaped by his world and culture. It doesn't seem like any religion, or any period of time, has the final say on life after death.

Jesus does talk a lot about the kingdom of Heaven, or the kingdom of God, which is right here, right now. He tells stories about how to live in this kingdom. He heals people, loves people, and makes room at the table for all the outsiders and losers in this world. He doesn't deny the existence of an afterlife, but it's not very important. Eternal life in the Gospels is a way of talking about the eternal life of God, of which we are all a part, which we can embrace in its fullness right now. The eternal life of God is flowing in and through all things. It's not way off in the future. To wake up to this is to live in the kingdom Jesus is talking about.

When I was fourteen, I stopped the push mower in the middle of the lawn. I turned off Bon Jovi's *New Jersey* tape on my Walkman, the classic yellow box of musical freedom. Then I started praying. I prayed the most genuine prayer I could pray. I prayed out loud, "God, I do not want to go to heaven. I don't want to go to hell. I just want to stop when all this is over. Is that possible? I want to disappear, to no longer exist. Can you make just one exception? I won't tell anyone." I can still feel the sun on my face as I think of it now, standing by the spruce tree. I can still feel my chest filling up with the courage to speak directly to God and beg for some other way of living, one without anxiety, fear, and threat.

Something was stirring in me that I couldn't name. For one thing, I couldn't fathom eternity—it was beyond my field of imagination. Who can? Most of us can hardly conceive of a 14.5-billion-year-old universe without some metaphors to help.

I was afraid of an eternal ocean of time—almost as much as I was afraid of the possibility of hell. And I was also entirely fed up with hearing about where I would go when I die. I couldn't handle any more speculation about streets of gold, or private mansions, or playing football and grilling kosher dogs with the Messiah. There had to be a better way to live, a better way to fall asleep at night, a better reason to get out of bed in the morning.

In addition to being more interested in girls than God, I was starting to ask the questions that so many teenagers ask: What about those who don't make the heavenly cut? What about those who never had the right holy water, from the right holy man, or said the right prayer, at the right time, and really believed it, without any doubt? What about those who never heard of Jesus?

The quest for the right address in the afterlife often puts human beings in the driver's seat. We *believe* our way into eternity. We try to play by all the right rules in order to get a prize at the end. We keep our end of the bargain, so God will keep his. God essentially rewards us for being right. But this scheme actually leaves human beings firmly in control of who's in and who's out.

A VERY BRIEF HISTORY OF HEAVEN AND HELL

As best we can tell, the Hebrew people in the time of the

Old Testament didn't believe in an afterlife. There's no mention of it in the Torah, the first five books of the Bible. There's nothing about it in the stories of Israel's history. It's not at the tail end of the Ten Commandments. There's nothing in the sacred poems and psalms that mentions it. The people who followed the God of Abraham did so without any promises of eternal bliss. How did they manage?

The ancient Hebrews spoke of *Sheol*, the watery grave where the body-spirit rests. This was not hell or heaven. Sheol was for everyone, wicked or righteous, for everyone dies. It was more like a shadowy underworld of sleep. Late in the biblical period, a couple of Hebrew prophets began to speak of a final judgment and seem to hint at life after death, or an age of lasting peace.[1] During this period, Greek and Zoroastrian ideas about eternity probably influenced the evolving Hebrew religion. Notions of death and eternity were not static but constantly evolving. Very slowly, ideas about resurrection, judgment, and paradise appeared within Judaism.

In Jesus's day, it was a convoluted mess. The ancient Hebrew religion had evolved into what could be called early Judaism, or more accurately Judaisms. Different expressions of the Jewish religion and different beliefs floated around in the air. Jewish groups loved to argue about what will happen in the end, both in terms of God's rule on earth and the afterlife. This lively conversation was anything from definitive. Emerging Rabbinic Judaism spoke of "the world to

---

1. For an accessible treatment on the evolution of hell, see Jon M. Sweeny, *Inventing Hell: Dante, the Bible, and Eternal Torment* (New York: Jericho Books, 2014).

come," but provided almost zero details. The Sadducees in contrast, who were the priestly establishment, don't appear to have believed in "the world to come." So even heaven was a matter of debate.

And hell? There is no mention of it in the Old Testament, no place of eternal torment for God's enemies. The New Testament word *Gehennah*, which has often been translated as hell, was a trash heap outside of Jerusalem. It was also the place where the wicked kings of Israel sacrificed their own sons to a foreign god. It's a place associated with darkness and evil. *Gehennah* was a picture of life without God. It was a picture of life outside the kingdom of heaven, right here and now. Being thrown into *Gehennah* was a dramatic image meant to shake people back to their true identity in God, a place of wholeness and beauty.

Most of the dramatic images of divine torture and abuse lodged in the contemporary Christian imagination actually come from the Italian poet Dante and Italian art, not the Bible. In fact, the church father Origen, the most influential person in the early church prior to Augustine, imagined that not even Satan would be able to resist the love of God. Hell was not permanent for anyone—not Judas, not Satan, and certainly not any of us. This is a metaphoric hint that the meaning of hell is not about permanent location but about what happens in the soul when it chooses separation from the love that gave it birth.

The history of hell also tells us a great deal about the human psyche, particularly the shadow side of that psyche. Hell is where we shove things that are elements of what we have a hard time facing in ourselves, putting these elements on the "other." We deny being anything like "them." We put our own shadow qualities on other people, or entire groups. This is the reason we hear about a preacher who rails against homosexuality, condemning gay people to hell, only to find out that he is gay. When we throw others into hell, we pretend we are nothing like them, we feign superiority. It's just easier to separate ourselves than to say, "What I hate in them I see in myself." If we did this kind of hard inner work, we would see the world as Jesus did. We would see there are no outsiders, no one left to condemn, like the woman caught in adultery. "Has no one condemned you?" asks Jesus. "Then neither do I."

I came to learn that most of the ancient speculations about the afterlife had more to do with justice than with eternal destiny. People imagined that God would put the world to rights, for the living and the dead. Images of a final judgment were meant to change present behavior. They were meant to bring the eternal rule of God into the present. The Hebrew prophets in particular were experts in wildly intense threats in order to provoke radical change. To push the prophetic threat into the future is to miss the point in this life. *Now* is the time for justice. *Now* is the time for peace. *Now* is time for God's eternal reign. The opposite is to burn in hell right now, a hell of our own making.

The Bible isn't really the source of our Christian obsession with the afterlife anyway. It was Plato who argued the soul was immortal and lived on. Moses never separated the soul from the body. But Plato influenced Paul as much as the

64

Torah. The Greeks were well down the road of imagining an eternal city for the immortal soul long before Paul or the early Christians. Paul's line, "to die is gain," was first uttered by Socrates in Plato's *Apologia*.[2]

As Christianity became more and more Greek, the vision of a separate soul, and that soul's eternal destiny, became a fixation, and that led to some unhelpful certainties about eternal destiny. To return to Jesus on the matter is to return to the kingdom of heaven in the here and now. In my view, we have gone far enough in speculating about our eternity. Like the rabbi said, it's not an important question.

The "world to come" is a mystery. This is a gift, not a curse. This frees us up to live in the here and now.

LOSING MY TASTE FOR THE AFTERLIFE

One Sunday after giving a sermon, a man waited in line to speak with me near the edge of the stage. He waited till the line had cleared out, then after shaking my hand, he asked, "Do you believe in a literal hell?" I looked at him and said, "No." He shifted his weight and shook his head. He repeated the question several times. I kept telling him I didn't believe in literal hell, not that I have the definitive word on the matter. He said a few nasty things and then he said something very revealing: "If there's no literal hell, there's no point to any of this." And we parted ways.

I think Moses would disagree, so would Jesus. But for a

2. To be fair, we don't have writing from the Sadducees. We only have texts written by their rivals, so we don't know what they believed in their own words.

lot Christians in my tradition, faith is about someone losing and someone winning. And the losers don't just lose, they're tortured.

The afternoon with the rabbi provoked a serious change in my life, in my spiritual geography. I set down some more unneeded baggage. I couldn't bring myself to argue about the afterlife anymore. I had no taste for it. If I was going to be religious in any obvious way, my spiritual life had to be about the present. I didn't care anymore where I was going or where anyone else was going. It's not an important question.

My dad came to visit me in Israel shortly after my chat with the rabbi. It was a joy to take him to class and to my favorite cafés. The physical manifestations of his ALS diagnosis were now obvious. I think we both wondered if this was his last visit to Jerusalem. On a walk one day, I told him that I no longer believed in an afterlife. Typically he laughed after my big announcements, but this time he only smiled. He said, "When you face death, you will." This was a little ominous for a man who liked to keep things light. But that was just it; heaven and hell seemed irrelevant as I watched his body shut down. And the thought of heaven was no comfort at all.

Death pushes against our theological certainties. Our level of confidence about what's next won't stave off the inevitable reality that this life ends. At his funeral, one friend of my father's announced, "We know that death is not real." What a bitter delusion! One thing we actually know is that death is very real.

In fact, my father's death came as a gift in the end. It was an ending of a life, an ending of his suffering, and an ending to one man's failures and successes at loving the only life he was given. What I trust is that the same love that gifted us life, gifts us death as well. What lies beyond is up to love. These are words of faith, as best I can get them out.

After his funeral I walked into the woods behind the house. The deep snow and the midnight glow of the winter forest seemed to welcome the indescribable strangeness of burying my father in the ground. I staggered around, crying as hard as I can remember crying. I let my body do what it wanted instead of holding back. I didn't know what I was doing in the woods, or why I'd come out here. I stumbled into a hardwood grove, my tears falling in the snow. In front of me was a dead tree, one I'd never noticed, broken in the middle, wrapped in a fungus of knots, probably the thing that choked out its life. I had this feeling that I was seeing my father.

I spoke to him, telling him the things I never got to say at his deathbed. I coughed and cried, leaning against the bark, as if this were the most natural thing in the world. I was surprised by the intensity of emotion. I thought the slow dying of a man had prepared me for tossing soil on his coffin, but it had not.

After a time my body grew still. I wasn't cold in the bitter night air. The forest was as silent as an abandoned monastery. I looked up at the trees, this forest of grandfathers who bore witness to my own grief. The trees that were here before I was born, and would live long after my own death, seemed to be holding a space for me. I felt seen in a way I'd felt unseen by my own father. And the grief was a gift from an unknown reservoir. I'd been afraid of going numb and remaining closed after his body returned to its home, so having a good cry felt life-giving and a bit of a relief.

It's very hard to describe in words what moved through my heart and soul in those mysterious moments. Was it a thought? Or a voice? Where did it come from: my psyche, or the earth, or the spirit of God? But I did know, in a way I'd never known before, that death is not a problem. Sad, yes, but not a problem. These words came out of my mouth, spoken to the forest, and to the broken tree, having been cut off too soon. My eyes filled with tears again. I thanked the forest itself and the December night, for I knew, in a very shy and simple way, I would never be the same again.

Death is not a problem. Death is a sobering gift. All things end. Of this we can be certain, even if we are uncertain if death is the beginning of something unknown. My dad's life, the only life he was given, was over. "The Lord gives and the Lord takes away." This is an ancient Hebrew poem about the way things are, not a philosophical statement about God as the causal agent of suffering, death, or even joy. All is given, all is taken. The universe breathes in, and the universe breathes out.

LETTING GO

I cannot build an argument against the existence of the

afterlife. Who am I to say what's going to happen? To be certain there is an afterlife and to be certain there is not an afterlife are pretty much the same thing. Agnosticism about the "world to come" is a more gracious and honest way of being spiritual for me.

I am actually talking about how to live more than metaphysical truths. I believe our imagination about what will happen is not benign. If we think Jesus will take all the good people to heaven and torture everyone else, there's no need to do anything other than worry about being in the right group. So much of Christianity is stuck right here. And what we believe about what's next makes a huge difference in our values, economics, politics, and spirituality. If other people are going to burn forever as the enemies of God, why love them? If God cannot love his enemies, neither should we. God cannot even practice what he preaches.

My own childhood theology, forged in the fires of being in the right group, had to come off the back of the camel in order to go any further. I had to let go of the reward/punishment, us vs. them, universe of eternal fear. There is a better way to live.

Let's worry about the afterlife, after life.

Let's relinquish the immature attachments of being in the right group. Let's let go of our thirst for immortality. That's the sin of Adam and Eve. We have yet to really let the gift of being human come out of hiding, "From dust you came and to dust you shall return." We can loosen our grip on the certainty of our eternal destiny.

This is a letting go more than a denial. This kind of

prayer is about opening our hands. It is about receiving rather than proclaiming, and certainly not about condemning. To let go of our certainty is to move a little more into being human, which is the point of all healthy spiritual practices. To feel it slip through the fingers frees us up to live now.

It is deeply spiritual to say, "I'm not sure." It is holy to say, "I don't really care." It is downright prophetic to say, "It's not an important question."

To actually live like this is to live a little closer to Jesus. "Do not worry about tomorrow, for today has enough trouble of its own," Jesus said. We've done almost nothing more than worry about the future. We've rarely taken Jesus at his word. Maybe it's time.

A seismic shake-up in our collective spiritual terrain is happening. And the afterlife is part of the shift. Promises of eternal torture and eternal paradise are not enough to keep many of us in the fold anymore. In fact, a God who needs a place like hell to put all the unbelievers is actually increasing the mass migration away from church.

After we walked silently for a few moments, the rabbi said to me, "'The world to come' is not my problem, that's God's problem." So let's give it over to God, whatever God may mean to you. It's simply not our concern. Let's pursue the fullest life we can have right now. This is the future of faith.

5

BEYOND BIBLE WORSHIP

On a field study with my classmates one afternoon, we sat enjoying the view of the Mount of Olives in Jerusalem. Many days we couldn't get over the fact that this place was our classroom. The limestone walls glowed in the winter sunlight, and I felt grateful to be in this crazy and magical place. Then my friend Keith asked quietly, "Do you think the ascension of Jesus was literal?"

We looked at the mountain, covered in tombs and hotels and churches. We could almost see it, hands down by his side, the first jetpack liftoff, shooting up through the clouds, beyond the gravitational pull of earth, up, up, and away. But did this event really happen? Are we allowed to even ask this question? Where did he go after passing through the clouds? And then we burst out laughing, feeling slightly guilty.

This is what Israel will do to you, if you let it. The actual places dismantle something of the literal ground on which we think our faith resides, a so-called faith that is grounded in facts. Some think faith is about believing that actual events happened exactly as the biblical text claims. And if the events didn't happen exactly the way the Bible says, then everything is untrue, right down the slippery slope we go, and at the bottom, there is no God.

But this kind of either-or dualism stopped working for me in Israel, where you can feel totally amazed to be standing where the ancient stories actually took place and also start to ask what actually took place. One site can confirm the stories in the Bible; another calls the whole thing into question. There really is a city called Jericho, one of the oldest cities in the world. But there's no archeological evidence of a serious destruction layer—tumbling walls—from the time period of Joshua. And this a major story in the Bible. But a few miles north, the destruction layer of the city of Hatzor, which the Bible claims was also destroyed by Joshua, seems to line up pretty well. It means that the stories and the historical events don't always match. The tour guides will not tell you the archeological and historical truth, at least not all of it, and this creates a lot of tension. It means that either the Bible is not reliable or that our understanding of what the Bible actually is needs to change. I vote for the latter.

Everywhere I went in Israel, I wondered what the "Word of God" meant. I wondered what sort of truth the Bible really contained. I wondered what kind of spiritual authority it held, especially since its historicity was shaky. After getting beaten up in the classroom and the field, most of my fellow students realized the limits of a Bible that's supposed to be historical, literal, infallible, and inerrant, as so many of us had been taught. Some stopped believing in God altogether the moment the Bible lost its solid ground. For me, I came to the end of being "Bible believing." I had to start admitting how little faith I actually had. This felt odd because my spiritual curiosity kept waxing as the beliefs of traditional evangelical theology kept waning.

Biblical inerrancy was invented in 1913. Just over a hundred years ago, a few Christians declared that the Bible was without error in every respect, including historically and scientifically. Catholics responded in kind by claiming papal infallibility. Both churches were backed into a corner by science, and both panicked. This did tremendous harm to the Bible and to our understanding of spiritual authority. To claim human literature and man-made institutional figures are without error and infallible is silly and embarrassing.

A few weeks after the ascension incident, I went to a lecture by an Orthodox Jewish scholar on the book of Jonah. He turned the story inside out in a clever rabbinic way, arguing that those who first read this story would've been rooting for Jonah, wanting Jonah to get as far away from Nineveh, and from God, as he possibly could. The people of Nineveh, the Assyrians, were the enemies of Jews. They destroyed all ten tribes of the Northern Kingdom of Israel. If Jonah went to Nineveh, told the city to repent, and then they repented, God would not destroy them. Jonah was a hero for running from God. The readers were probably hoping God would go ahead and destroy the city. The surprise, which sent Jonah into an unresolved depression at the end of the story, is that God apparently cares for all people. I loved every minute and felt as if I'd never even read the story before.

Then he said something very subtle, almost as an aside. "Of course Jonah is a story. He wasn't really swallowed by a fish."

"What?" I wondered. "How can an Orthodox Jew believe the story is not factual?" Apparently, being a person of deep faith and a critical scholar is not a contradiction. Apparently, the truth of the Bible wasn't in its historicity or in its scientific certainty. I thought, "If he can be a person of faith, I have no idea what faith really is. It must not be about believing certain things about the Bible or certain claims in the Bible." The book at the center of my religious world was falling apart. I'd learned how to worship the Bible instead of what the Bible only points to.

KISSING THE BIBLE (GOODBYE?)

I've been in and out of love with the Bible most of my life. I've gone through all the ups and downs of a rocky relationship, like breaking up and getting back together with your first real love. I directed a lot of my unprocessed pain toward the Bible, and my own unclarified longings. The first real personal questions I had around faith started with the text: What does it say? Why does it say it? What does it mean? How are we to make sense of it? What did it mean in its original context? Most of my professional life, my teaching and writing have been swirling around the text. I don't regret any of this wild ride. Every time I dug deeper into the text, the deeper the bottom seemed to be. It also gave me loads of trouble.

My hang-ups with the Bible are as old as my memory. In the second grade, my teacher at Falwell's school lined us up in front of the Bible, which she placed on a desk at the back of the classroom. She gave us the choice to either kiss it or spit on it, telling us that kids in Communist China were given the same choice, and they were shot if they chose to kiss it. She wanted to know if we would we die for our faith. I dutifully kissed the Bible, mouth tightly clenched in confusion, imagining a gun to my head.

My first exposure to the Bible engendered anxiety, even though we were told that God loved us and gave his Word to live by. Before we formed any questions of our own, we were taught that the Bible had all the answers. God talked to us through his special word, a how-to book for life. If we had any questions, we could look in the concordance at the back of the Bible and find a verse for every question. And it did seem to have all the answers; at least to the questions we were supposed to be asking. But fear and anxiety and "right" answers don't make for a healthy relationship.

I know many people have moved on, have given up on the Bible altogether. I understand. Sometimes giving up is the only way for something new to happen. Like the twelve-step program, we admit we are powerless in our ability to work things out. But our culture hasn't really moved on. The Bible, a messy and misunderstood book, continues to shape our parenting, school systems, politics, entertainment, and our churches. Politicians and pop stars and pastors keep quoting and misquoting the Bible. Athletes think it gives them strength. It won't go away, even though most of us cannot answer the simple question, "What is it?"

The Bible is a collection of books, edited and written over hundreds of years, in three ancient languages. It contains multiple genres, from poetry to song to history to myth to parable to letters and more. The language, at many points, is mythopoetic.

I mean something specific by myth. A myth is a way of telling the truth that is richer than just facts. A myth is a story that's true but not historical. It's concerned with the symbolic, archetypal, and metaphoric. In a good myth we find something of our own lives being reflected back to us. This is absolutely true of the biblical stories.

And poetry is the language of the heart, or the soul, which points to a deeper reality than words can convey. Poetry loves image and sound. In the Bible, God is a shepherd, a stone, a snare, a lover, a midwife, a fire, and a whirlwind. He is a name that cannot be spoken easily without sounding like you're breathing, *Yahweh*. Pure poetry. A mythopoetic text speaks deep truths in words that point beyond themselves. I think this is what makes the Bible so enduring and provocative. But so often, we treat it as an answer book to ward off all ambiguity.

In my final year as the teaching pastor at Mars Hill, many of the conversations with the church elder board had to do with the "same-sex question," and it was breaking us apart.

At the time, we sincerely believed that different interpretations could coexist at the same leadership table. We thought this happened with other questions of faith, so maybe it could happen with this contentious one. Many of the key staff supported an open and affirming position toward our gay brothers and sisters. Many of the pastors were willing to perform gay marriages, before gay marriage was even legal. But most of the elders did not support such positions. It was hard to believe that the ship we boarded was heading in any particular direction.

We attempted to hold several opposing positions at the same time. We called this a "third way," where we could avoid taking a public position, where diversity of opinion was tolerated. We entered the conversation with seriousness, ready to comb through every verse in the entire Bible (all six of them). The pastoral staff went to work providing summaries of key positions taken, defining Greek words and presenting the various interpretations, from traditional to progressive. There was a steep learning curve for all of us. I'd just finished editing the NIV First Century Study Bible, so I was neck deep in research and footnotes. You would think that I was equipped to be wading into the muddy waters of interpretation. But I felt lost.

My working assumption was that ambiguity opens doors. I thought that if we really drilled down to the complexities of the ancient language, the cultural background, and so forth, the obvious ambiguities would soften people. We would all say, "It's not that clear, so let's relax. Let's trust grace and compassion. Let's not dare call anyone a 'sinner,' or label another person as flawed." I thought that giving people different interpretive possibilities for contentious texts would bring more openness. But I was wrong. It actually seemed to entrench people. The thirst for biblical certainty kept us from getting anywhere. Biblical certainty kept getting in the way and we didn't know how to move beyond it.

So much of what passes as biblical certainty boils down to taste. "I like my interpretation," we say (without saying it). "My interpretation is better than yours, because it is clear, right here, the way I read it. Therefore it's right." Back and forth it goes. There is no way out of this spin cycle. We end up gripping tightly to our interpretive convictions, believing they're the very words of God, as if we're doing God a favor. Though we were leading a megachurch, the truth was we had no agreement on how to hold the very thing at the center of our faith: the Bible.

And I wondered what a book was doing at the center of our faith in the first place.

Something's happening in our struggle with the text that's subtle. If the Bible really doesn't confirm all our presumptions (which it doesn't), then we ignore it, or do a lot of interpretive gymnastics to make it fit. For example, most women come to church with their heads uncovered, some in braids; they wear gold, and they talk in church instead of asking their husbands questions at home, all of which Paul bans. We tend to eat meat with blood in it, which an entire council of Christians in Jerusalem forbids. Some of us circumcise our kids, which Paul argues is worthless and that we might as well cut the whole thing off. At our church we broke with the traditional and historic view of women in leadership but did not break with the traditional view of marriage. My point is, we all live with glaring inconsistencies when it comes to the Bible. We make the Bible do our bidding and then refuse to admit it.

When I give sermons, I try to say something true, something real. This is what most pastors do, as best they can. It's a hard job, no matter what your theology. Most pastors I know feel uneasy about what they do, and here's why: There's not some definitive guide for doling out the truth. We all know, when we read the Bible, there are several possible interpretations. We know we don't actually speak for God, we're only looking for clues. We also know the history of Christian orthodoxy is a rocky road of political agendas, power grabs, and violent opposition to any voice not toeing the line. What passes as "orthodox" is a human construct made by a patriarchal hierarchy of political power. We know that the acceptable images of God have more to with cultural norms that anything else. Most of us learned all this in graduate school or through our own honest reading of Christian history. But it's really hard to admit all this in public!

The Bible is too often a concrete substitute for God. We put our faith in the words, probably because we can hold it in our hands. But this can actually block us from the divine, instead of opening us up. When we substitute the text for the divine, everything depends upon the correct reading. This happens to liberals and conservatives alike. We think if we get our reading right, with the right interpretive lens, it will reveal to us the road to meaning, or to heaven, or to God. We're really worshiping the words, and our unstated interpretative convictions about the words, instead of the divine mystery to which the words only point.

We're suffering from a systemic loss of imagination around the Bible and an erosion of mythic meaning, a language the Bible speaks well. We're suffering under our own self-imposed curse, that to tell the truth one must be literal, historic, and scientific, categories the Bible knows very little about. Or on the other extreme, we tend to think of the Bible as full of cute metaphors from long ago that don't really tell us anything important. Both of these positions degrade the power of some of the richest stories ever told.

I've come to trust that the stories are not asking us to believe them, but to engage them. For example, we don't allow ourselves to disagree with Paul. Or after hearing Jesus say, "Love your neighbor as yourself," we don't ask, together with the teacher of law in the story, "Who is my neighbor?" We leave our questions at home, when in fact they are needed to open up to new ways of seeing.

One late afternoon, as my rabbinic Judaism class let out, the rabbi asked us to read the story of Abraham binding his son Isaac when we got home. He asked us to make a list of questions as our only assignment. I went home dutifully, knowing how much he loved a good question. The rabbi taught the class with a twinkle in his eye and constantly apologized to the Christians for anything offensive he said about Jesus, a rabbi whom he respected. A few weeks under his spell and I realized how much Judaism thrived on questions and dialogue, so I wanted to do my best to find the inconsistencies and ambiguities in the story.

We all came to class prepared. After we shared, which took a few minutes, he looked at each of us and said, "That's it? That's all you have? You are so lucky! I read this story and I have more questions than all of you combined. None of you even challenged God. You can accept a God who asks a father to kill his son, in the name of God? I cannot accept this."

I shook my head in disbelief. Is this allowed? I wondered. We can actually question God and not just the text? We can challenge the divine? The answer, I gathered from my professor, is "Yes!" And now, for me, to be spiritually alive means bringing all our questions to the table. We aren't asked to blindly accept anything. The text is meant to stir our curiosity and our questions, not shut them down or give us all the answers like a test that's already been filled out by the teacher.

It's not the Bible's fault. It's the preconceived expectations we brought to the relationship that's the problem. That's what we need to shed.

WHAT THE BIBLE IS, AND IS NOT

The people who wrote and edited the Bible didn't know they were working on the Bible. There was no Bible, no obsession with the truth being confined to words on a page. Paul wasn't hoping his letters would make the cut for the

New Testament canon. He might have laughed at words like *inerrant* and *infallible*. He spoke from his experience, for better and for worse.

The collection of books that were eventually bound together is a beautiful mess. It's "useful for teaching," as Peter asserts. But it is not the "word of God" in the way we think. In fact, the Bible never claims to be the "word of God." It's full of words written about God, and about love and suffering and death and war and family, by people who were trying to figure life out, make sense of their experiences and tell stories. And this is where the truth really resides, in the muddled mess.

Like all good poetry and myth, the Bible is meant to work on us, over time, slowly, like a stream over a riverbed. It creates a longing in us for contact with God, and then leaves us unfulfilled and ready for the real thing. The church father Origen says, "Daily we read the scriptures and experience a dryness of soul until God grants food to satisfy the soul's hunger."[1] Real food doesn't come straight from the page. It's like something happens in the soul, between the lines on the page. When we read, "As the deer pants for streams of water, so my soul pants for you, O God," we pant for something beyond the words. The language simply activates or deepens our own longing. And so the Bible calls us more deeply into our own experience, in all its naked reality.

The Bible gives us stories of setting forth, like Abraham, but we must walk out ourselves. It gives us a law, knowing

---

1. See Henry Chadwick, *Early Christianity* (London: Penguin, 1993).

we will come to the limits of any law, and start the real journey. It sings songs of longing and loss and love, which only awaken in us our own senses of the same. It's sometimes judgmental and tribal, which reveals a bit of what's true in our psyches, whether we admit it or not. We think it will tell us something definitive about God, but it gives away only hints, guesses, and images.

As we walk into the desert of our own lives, like Israelites leaving Egypt, the Bible gives us a few fragments of a map from long ago, with a few wrong turns and hidden treasures.

The great patterns of truth in the text reflect back to us something we recognize when we get honest about what it's like to be human. This is true with all mythopoetic stories, with all the best sacred texts. This is a realm of subtlety, not a world where God tells us what to think and what to believe. This is a world where quiet and contemplation are needed, not word studies and definitions.

My own questions about the Bible have changed dramatically over the last few years. I rarely ask anymore, "What does this passage mean?" or "What is God really trying to say?" More often I'm asking, "What effect does this passage or story have on me? What am I drawn to or repulsed by?" I learned these new questions from a very ancient practice known as *lectio divina*, or divine reading, which is being rediscovered by all kinds of spiritual seekers. Listening to a passage, very slowly, often out loud, and allowing a word or phrase to draw me in, or capture my attention, is at the heart of this practice.

I've found that allowing a phrase or word to work deeply is more humble way of engaging the sacred stories. It assumes the powerful symbols, images, phrases, questions, and stories can change us, when we allow them to wash over us. We are in fact, not in control of the sacred movements. We are drawn to different elements of the story from wherever we are in life, from our own hang-ups and prejudices, to our own hopes and longings. It's like the story shines its light into the circumstances of our lives in different ways at different times. That's where the magic happens, where the Spirit or Wind of the God stirs.

DESERT VOICES

In the fourth century, an old man came to see the desert monk Abba Anthony and his followers.

> In the midst of them was Abba Joseph. Wanting to test them, the old man suggested a text from the scriptures, and, beginning with the youngest, he asked them what it meant. Each gave his opinion, as he was able. But to each one the old man answered, "You have not understood." Last of all he said to Abba Joseph, "How would you explain this saying?" and he replied, "I don't know." Then Abba Anthony said, "Indeed, Abba Joseph has found the way, for he said, 'I don't know.'"[2]

2. Helen Waddell, *Desert Fathers* (Ann Arbor: University of Michigan Press, 1972), 116.

The desert fathers lead the way here. A fair amount of "I don't know" is needed to shed the heavy burden of a particular view of the Bible so many of us have been carrying.

My archeology professor used to say with a sly grin that the Bible is like a cake. It's not, "none of this stuff happened," or "all of this stuff happened." Whether it "happened" is not really important. There are all kinds of ingredients in the cake: poetry, myth, legend, history, editorial insertions, scribal errors and agendas. We're not sure how much of each ingredient was used. And we'll never know. "The recipe is lost," he'd say in his thick and hard-to-place accent. But I've found that it still came together to make something worth savoring. And this is what makes the Bible so interesting and rewarding. It's a deeply spiritual book, an ancient literary masterpiece, and a guide into the depths of the human experience.

The kind of reading I'm arguing for makes the Bible more rich, wild, beautiful, human, and sacred. Who of us does not live in our own mess of contradictions and flashes of clarity? So we can expect to see as much reflected back to us in the text. Like Pilate we must ask, "What is truth?" We ask this of the stories and more importantly we ask this of ourselves. This makes us participants, not spectators, or robots of doctrinal certainty, or iconoclasts bent on dismantling the Bible.

In the meetings with the church leadership, we found no way out of the muck of biblical authority and certainty. There was little transformation of thought or shift in opinion. We actually regressed by clinging too tightly to the page. Gay people remained second-class spiritual citizens, welcome to attend our church, but little more. A "moratorium" on gay marriage was instituted that was never lifted, and openly gay people were not allowed to serve at the highest levels. In an attempt to pursue a third way, our gay brothers and sisters lost, while the traditional position gave up nothing, and suffered nothing.

Though we tried, not every position was really honored in our attempt to honor different convictions. And by not taking a public position, the "third way" ended up being a way to quietly sweep the hard stuff under the rug. Gay people remained in the lower category of "sinners" for many—ironically the very category of people Jesus hung out with—while we talked about them behind closed doors with the Bible in hand. To tell you the truth, none of us felt good about this, but we had little imagination for another way to hold the scriptures.

We ended up worshiping the golden calf of biblical certainty, instead of the mysterious, compassionate, inclusive, and untamed God to which the text only points. In fact, the text speaks of spiritual authority coming from a different, inner source. Jeremiah says we will "all be taught by God." Jesus says the Spirit will "guide us into truth." He also says the living water of God "will flow from within."

In my experience, to lean toward these images of inner authority requires a different and deeper faith because it's really hard to make definitive and absolute statements about what this inner welling up is really about. The divine indwelling in all of us can't be pinned down. The only litmus test that seems to make sense for the divine indwelling is whether or not we are dropping our judgments, radically loving other people, and being people of inclusive justice. It's hard to trust anything else if we claim that Jesus is our teacher in any concrete way.

In fact, the Bible itself was never a big fan of definitive authority, especially spiritual authorities. It levels criticism every time the system becomes too closed. The Bible turns over its own tables. It rages against religious rules, internal corruption, the temple, the priesthood, the rich, and the establishment. The very book we look to, that we hold up as our source of external authority, challenges our ideas about external authority.

Isaiah calls the keeping of the Sabbath and the festivals "abhorrent," speaking for God and in contrast to the Ten Commandments. Jeremiah mocks the public attachment to "the Temple, the Temple, the Temple," something the text instructs the people to build. David says the real sacrifices to God are a "broken and contrite heart," instead of the sacrificial system. Jesus pokes fun of the tithes and offerings of the religiously faithful, while they neglect justice and mercy. In their defense, they were just following the Bible. The prophetic voices have no palate for the games of institutional devotion, confining God to a page, or reducing spirituality to rule keeping.

It's as if the external systems, or the words themselves, were simply placeholders. They held our hands till we could feel the movement of the divine welling up in our own hearts. When this divine indwelling happens, we actually have a worthy conversation partner with the words of the Bible. We have something to rub against, as iron sharpens iron. But the divine indwelling, the Spirit, is a wild wind that knocks over barriers and walls. We should expect resistance from the institutional gatekeepers and to feel at odds with certain passages of the Bible. All is well and good.

This is the way of Jesus that I find so compelling. He empowers his own followers to trust their convictions and the fresh movement of the mystery of God when he says, "Whatever you bind on earth will be bound in heaven, whatever you loose on earth will be loosed in heaven." He seems to give away this kind of power rather than create more controls. And in case we need some guardrails on this permissive road, Jesus also says the entire law can be summed up with the words, "Do unto others as you would have them do unto you." This means our convictions are kept in check by our practice first and foremost. The hard part, at least for me, is to really live this simple teaching, instead of trying to explain it. Living it is to interpret the Bible correctly, at least according to Jesus.

This kind of faith requires a lot of humility and a deep trust that the mystery of God is still at work, is not confined to a book, or to the traditional interpretations of that book. Perhaps what's needed right now, as we venture out further, is a little of Saint Ephrem's fourth-century approach to the text, "I took my stand halfway between love and awe."

6

ENDING END TIMES AND COMING BACK TO EARTH

I wandered into an Anglican church one Sunday morning, not too far from Damascus Gate in Jerusalem. I'd never been, and I heard the building was worth seeing. A stunning stained-glass window of an olive tree stretches above the apse. In the center of the room, where the altar once stood, were microphones and electrical chords and a worship band. The music had already started when I snuck in the back. Dancing, ribbon waving, and the sound of a tambourine shaking bounced around the ordinarily silent stone walls. These were happy people, glad to have a church filled with believers, in the most religious city on earth.

We were singing a simple refrain, "There will be more with us than there will be with them." The energy was building, the song was getting louder, ribbons where flying about. The preacher injected a few mini-sermons over the music. "Very soon, any day now, Jesus is going to come back." A few cheers and shouts went up. "He will appear on the Mount of Olives." Clapping and "Amens" filled the church. "His face will light up this very stained glass and the rapture will begin." Hands went up in the air. "Our forefathers built this window with this glorious day in mind. And now it is almost here." Tambourine solos and more singing.

"On that day, there will be more with us than there will be with them. More with us than with them! It will all be over." The room swayed. "Jesus will draw all the Jews to his glorious light." The truth was coming out. "Anyone who rejects the presence of Jesus, the enemies of God, will finally get what they deserve. His foot will land so hard on the Mount of Olives, there will be an earthquake. We will feel it right here in this church. The second coming of Christ is going to happen any day now. For us, it will be a day of glory, and we will all join Christ in the air. For everyone else, it will be a day of judgment." Shouts and cheers. "There will be more with us than there will be with them."

I walked out of the church, blinded by the afternoon light, feeling nauseated and disturbed. This preaching about the rapture, where Jesus whisks away all the Christians and then systematically destroys those left behind suddenly felt like a spiritual cancer. I couldn't swallow this fearful vision of the future anymore. I'd been telling myself that it didn't really matter what anyone believed about "the end." But I was wrong. Our stories about what will happen here on this earth, in the near future, are absolutely essential. They affect our politics, what we consume, how we treat the earth and our neighbor.

I also felt guilty, like I couldn't stand outside of all this stuff anymore, keep it all at arm's length, no matter how hard I tried. It was just as much my problem as everyone inside the church. The tradition I inherited, like it or not, had some really dangerous hopes for the future.

A Jesus who is going to burn and torture everyone who doesn't accept his earth-quaking return is not a messenger of love and not in line with Jesus of Nazareth as portrayed in the Bible. This theological tribalism divides the world up between the truly worthy and everyone else. Singing happy songs that express our hope that Jesus will come and destroy this earth and everyone on it so we can get a brand-new one for all the people in our tribe is, to be frank, sick. It's not only wishful thinking, but it doesn't honor the reality that the earth we have right now, not to mention the people on it, is already infused with the divine.

Even the so-called "love" of Israel by many Christians has very little to do with real people. I know this firsthand, having been around dozens of people and organizations in Jerusalem proclaiming their devotion to Israel. But sadly, the Jews in Israel are often pawns in an endgame where all the Christians will win and get to live to Israel, while the unbelievers get screwed, including the "unbelieving Jews."

I grew up with all this. The Moral Majority was fueled by this kind of End Times thinking. I heard countless sermons about the rapture and the political clues that the end was near. My dad even wrote a book giving twenty-one reasons why Jesus might return before the year 2000. After Y2K I asked him if now was a good time to read the book. He laughed, shaking his head, and said, "You're bad, son, you're bad," his go-to line for not wanting to talk about it.

As kids, we were on high alert for the rapture, our free ride out of here. We believed that at any moment we would be sucked up to heaven, accompanied by a trumpet blast. We were afraid of the Russians, one world currency, the mark of the beast, bar codes, and credit cards. These were signs the end was near. At school we practiced crouching under our desks in case of nuclear war, a pretty weak attempt to survive such a nightmare. We were told that the rapture might happen before or after the nuclear bombs started falling, so best to be prepared. It was a terrifying way to grow up.

Something really changed for me as I reflected on what I found so disturbing that Sunday morning, singing about the rapture. It wasn't just that it reminded me of my own fundamentalist upbringing. It seemed to me that certain beliefs about the world we live in feed these kinds of end-times expectations. Many of us have a pretty poor view of the world itself. The fact that we have so little concern for the destruction of life on this earth is rooted, in part, on Western Christian theological notions of a disposable and sinful world. In other words, the industrial revolution that viewed the earth as a bunch of abstract resources for our personal gain had years of theological support to build upon. It's not just about End Times and crazy preachers who predict the end of the world. It's about all of us, right here, on this earth.

I wanted so badly to outgrow all this, to reimagine life on this earth, and to enter a more faithful image of the future. I wanted to fall in love with the world, rather than hope to escape it. I don't believe the people singing songs like the ones we sang near Damascus Gate are bad people. They've just been blinded by hundreds of years of misunderstanding, as I have been. If we don't face together our own unhelpful eschatological hopes, our escapist visions of the "last things," we will meet our own fiery and destructive end. It won't be the feet of Jesus landing too hard on a mountain in Jerusalem but by our own weapons and waste and abuse of the earth. We'll create an apocalypse of our own making. Jesus isn't going to bail us out. For the first time in my life, I started probing deeper into my own convictions and hopes for the future. Up until Jerusalem, I just tried to ignore the whole thing. But this was one more layer that needed to be removed if I was going to move a little further into the unknown.

Maybe you've heard Einstein's famous line, "No problem can be solved by the same consciousness that created it." The consciousness I carried, that had specific views about our place on this earth, and the big story we were all in, couldn't generate a fresh and more hopeful vision. My whole way of thinking, particularly about our place on this planet, needed to shift. This is what I craved, a new consciousness. If consciousness sounds too fancy, I mean simply a new way of thinking, living, and being in the world.

A few weeks after this jarring encounter in the Anglican church I was in a class on ancient Jerusalem texts. We'd been reading all kinds of obscure passages, in many languages, trying to get a sense for the grand story of Jerusalem and the people who've called it home. One day, the teacher came to class and said she wanted to begin not with history, but with a poem. She held in her hands a poem by Yehudah Amichai, written in Hebrew. She began to read, very slowly, translating as she went. She held back tears as she tried to get the words out. Here is part of the poem in English.

The Tourists

Once I sat on the steps by a gate at David's City, I placed my two heavy baskets at my side. A group of tourists was standing around their guide and I became their target marker.

"You see that man with the baskets? Just right of his head is an arch from the Roman period. But he's moving, he's moving!" I thought to myself: redemption will come only if their guide tells them, "You see that arch from the Roman period? It's not important: but next to it, left and down a bit, there sits a man who's bought fruits and vegetables for his family."[1]

This is a future worth imagining, an eschatology rooted in our shared humanity, on the living earth. This is real

---

1. Yehuda Amichai, *The Selected Poetry of Yehuda Amichai* (Berkeley: University of California Press, 1996).

redemption, at least to me. I couldn't hold back my own tears in the middle of class. After a quiet cry, we all tried to get back to academic business, knowing we'd just brushed against the real business of our age.

THE POSTER

All the classrooms had a poster on the wall when I was a high school Religion teacher. The poster had four quadrants: creation, fall, redemption, and restoration. Each quadrant had a different artistic expression of these words. Creation looked peaceful, the fall dark and ominous, redemption an image of the cross, and restoration new life and a new earth. Because this was a Christian school, the poster provided a frame of reference for the grand story we're all in. And grand stories matter.

This theological grid was pretty typical Protestant Reformed theology. I grew up with some version of this map being drilled into my head. The big story was our linear passage through this fourfold path. A perfected creation, starting with Adam and Eve, was a thing of the past. We were somewhere post "fall," between "redemption" and "restoration."

But sometimes, when I referred to this poster in class, it didn't ring true for me in the way it always had. When Haiti was leveled by an earthquake, it seemed cheap and cruel to say, even in the most general terms, this kind of suffering was the result of the "fall" and that one day we'll all be living in a perfected world where nothing bad will ever happen. It turned out that lots of things couldn't be run through this grid. In fact, it started causing theological problems for me. For one thing, it didn't make sense to start with a perfect created order that Adam and Eve messed up. This didn't jibe with what was happening down the hall in science class.

Evolution, no matter what our convictions as teachers or the opinions of the students, had raised new questions. It seemed to throw off the beginning of the grand narrative. Starting in the wrong place meant the whole trajectory was off.

A few of my students had stopped believing in a literal Garden of Eden, surely horrifying their parents. I'd stopped as well, but I tried my best not to force my own views on the students. Merely considering the possibility there never was a literal Eden meant maybe there was no literal Fall. Death, hardship, and suffering couldn't be pinned on the actions of two human beings. If creation itself wasn't broken, or under some curse from the Fall, then maybe we didn't need a new creation at the end of days as many of us had been taught. It's like we were learning to ask again, assuming we didn't know the answers, "What is this world? And where are we heading?"

Evolution started changing my notions of God. The God I'd always imagined, that was part of the baggage I'd been carrying, was a clockmaker God, a being up in heaven, who made the world a few thousand years ago out of nothing. And according to the theological convictions we were singing about that morning in Jerusalem, this clockmaker is fashioning a new world for the believers at the end of time.

But the mechanistic sky God was dying for me. This God wasn't really like the mysterious *YHVH* or *ELOHIM* of the biblical creation poems in first place. The more I listened to the actual creation narratives, the more unscientific and nonliteral they seemed and also the more archetypal, symbolic, and truly powerful when read through another lens.

When it comes to evolution I don't think it's the scientific facts that most disturb the worldview I grew up with. The deeper fear is that we might have to rethink our God and admit how little we actually know rather than simply adjust the scientific data to fit our clockmaker God. I've felt this fear. More than once I've wanted to ask God, "What were you waiting for all those billions of years, and mass extinctions, and asteroid mishaps? Were you paying attention? Who are you?" Evolution messes with our worldview. We no longer seem to be the center of the universe anymore. But very slowly I realized that not being at the center of things could be embraced, along with the fear, dread, and wonder of it all. The needed shift in consciousness that Einstein hints at will not likely happen without it.

I've come to think of evolution itself as a kind of theology, an expression of God's word. Evolution gives us words for a beautiful, complex, and mysterious reality. Everything is morphing, changing, expanding, growing, collapsing, and renewing. I even think of words like creation, fall, redemption, and restoration as evolving right alongside everything else. Attempting to come to terms with evolution right now has been more important to me than believing in the virgin birth or the inerrancy of the Bible. It puts the human experiment in its rightful place. We can no longer assume God made the world just for us.

Thomas Aquinas said that when we make a mistake about creation, we make a mistake about God, and much of Western Christianity has made a big mistake. To say "no" to evolution, is to say "no" to God. It's like telling God that he should play by our rules because we're used to our sky-god images and don't want to change. To say "yes," is to enter a new freedom, to step toward a new consciousness that's greeting us at the door, and to behold new images of the divine.

Still, I can hardly watch programs on television about space or the origins of the earth without an existential freak-out. Such hard-to-fathom truth takes us right to the heart of mystery. And where else would God be located than mystery? We're drawn right into a place of wonder and gratitude. In fact, when I feel most alive I'm saying "thank you," even if I'm unsure what or who I'm thanking. Life is a mystery to be lived, not to be solved.

It took me a long time to really let go of my sky-god clockmaker. And he still creeps in from time to time. But it started in the seventh grade when I first heard about evolution in public school. My parents decided my faith was strong enough in Junior High to send me into the secular lion's den. But good thing it wasn't that strong. I can still remember the timeline my teacher put up on the board. I knew I wasn't supposed to believe it, at least according to my parents and my church. But a "God said it, I believe it, that settles it" didn't settle it for me.

Since then, I've been through every variation of trying to reconcile the Bible and science. I needed a lot of time to face the existential dismantling that evolution caused. But once all the negotiations were over, it was time to realize that my ideas of God had to go, not just my ideas about the universe. I couldn't keep doing theological gymnastics, trying to make a biblical text say something it doesn't. I couldn't pretend the story of creation, fall, redemption, and restoration explains everything important about life. It seems that a modified sacred story, a new grand narrative, is in order. The old one has served us well enough but it's now in the way.

I've come to believe that the actual universe story we're discovering is a new kind of sacred scripture.[2] These new realities are changing us; changing the church and our spiritual communities. There's no science-religion divide anymore. We have an opportunity now to get as curious about human biological evolution, quantum physics, anthropology, and space as we are about the meaning of the Eucharist. They're of equal theological significance. Our theology changes along with our cosmology, as it always has.

There's no need to throw out the Bible, in case anyone is worried. The Bible never entered the scientific conversation in the first place. There was no science when the poets finally wrote down the oral traditions passed around the family fires. And even the theological metaphors of cre-

---

2. See Brian Swimme and Thomas Berry, *The Universe Story: From the Primordial Flaring Forth to the Ecozoic Era—A Celebration of the Unfolding of the Cosmos* (New York: HarperOne, 1992).

ation, fall, redemption, and restoration predate our scientific revolution and don't need to be applied in any literal way to the physical universe.

A more honest view of creation is growing on the other side of our initial stabs at explaining how the world came to be. Creation is something that's happening, a dynamic emerging. The six days of creation, so to speak, are happening all the time. And accepting our infinitesimal speck of existence upon the ocean of 14.5 billion years requires a new humility. There's no need to march around as if we own the place. Apparently God didn't create all this stuff just to run us through creation, fall, redemption, and restoration, as if the world was just a prop for our escape to another, better world.

THE OTHER WORD OF GOD

The first word of God is *light*, according the Bible. This is in the opening paragraph. When we see the sun, it's as if we see a divine word. All of creation is spoken into being in this way, and everything is called good. Over the course of time, the entire language of God reverberates across the universe. In the beginning, the first word(s) of God, the first revelation of the divine, is reality itself. The unfolding—aka, evolving—of the universe is God learning to speak.

This is a profoundly sensitive worldview. Only a poet in love with creation, in love with nature, could have penned the opening chapter of Genesis. Only an experience of wonder could have given birth to such insight. The biblical storytellers were artists not scientists. Most of the biblical writers experienced and imagined a world where everything was alive with the presence of God. If we want to hear from God, according to them, we have but to listen to God's word(s) all around us.

This view of creation is also at the very heart of the Christian message. We claim that in Jesus, "The word became flesh." The word has always become something real. The physical world is the physical body of God, the divine word taking form. Why would we ever want a ticket out of this profound in-flesh-ment? This world *is* our home, the place where God takes on form.

I'm not convinced creation is broken, the way I was taught. We actually belong to the earth and are the earth. The particles in our body preceded their present arrangement and will outlast their present form. Creation is just fine, as it is, in all its diversity, complexity, and terrifying beauty. "For God so loved the world"—the Greek word for *world* in this overused verse is actually *cosmos*. When was the last time you heard of a Christian loving the cosmos? We might thank God *for* the cosmos. But to fall in love with the cosmos would be more God-like, and it would be to fall in love with the divine.

My wife and I once took the train to Assisi, the home of Saints Francis and Clare, while visiting our friends in Italy. We stood outside the small chapel that turned Saint Francis's life upside down, waiting for them to open after lunch. We decided to read aloud the Canticle of the Creatures to pass the time. As we read, the whole valley came alive. The sun shone bright, the olives glistened, the wind seemed kind, and the birds sang more beautifully than I had heard before. Something like love, or grace, moved through the hillside. The voice of Saint Francis rang in our hearts and came to life in everything around us. It felt like a pure gift, like I was seeing what was really true, all the time, but just hadn't noticed.

Saint Francis and Jesus of Nazareth embodied a natural spirituality. They discerned the invisible hand of God in all of earth's wild beauty. For Jesus, the lilies of the field were more beautiful than any man-made object. For Francis, the sun was his brother, the moon his sister. And it seems to me that this way of seeing is an important path back to our own sanity, with our two feet on the ground, a place we should be calling "home." They invite us back to a spiritual intimacy with the created order, the word of God all around us. Until we learn again that the sun is our brother, we will never know the kind of spiritual intimacy that's possible for our souls. We cannot love what we refuse to get to know, or what we abuse.

My most profound spiritual experiences have happened in nature, not in church. This seems to be the case with a lot of us. When I was nineteen, I got up in the middle of the night to pee while sleeping in the backcountry of Yellowstone National Park. Nothing is worse than getting out of your sleeping bag when it's 30 degrees, so I was annoyed and in a hurry. But I happened to look up at the stars on this clear night. They nearly knocked me over; my eyes filled with tears, I let out a gasp, and I could not get back to sleep for hours.

The Milky Way is a divine sentence, one that I had never read. Both saints and scientists insist we're deeply interconnected with all of reality, with the meadow and the far-flung reaches of space. This is a workable spirituality for this century.

Most people know this anyway, deep down, even if they wouldn't use my language. When we gather on a beach to watch the sunset, we feel a connection with the earth and the divine grace of life itself. When the first snowfall covers the grass, we smile and feel graced by something. When the robins return in the spring, and our hearts are moved with gratitude, we're actually feeling the sacredness and interconnection of the big story we're in. We're coming back home and back to life, as if we're simply the next sacred expression of the word of God.

THE HISTORICAL JESUS AND THE REAL SECOND COMING

I taught high school religion for six years at two different Christian schools. My students were surprisingly diverse—economically, racially, and theologically. I loved the real questions they asked and their creative alternatives to traditional theological answers. However, by the time my students reached high school, Jesus was an enigma. Maybe too much God-talk had obscured our vision and stunted our curiosity. They craved any story that challenged the nice-guy-god image that was so prevalent in our religious circles. And they were very suspicious of an angel-like deity who was going to appear in the sky to take us home.

I created an assignment one year to probe their ideas about Jesus of Nazareth. I had students bring in different images of Jesus until we filled the classroom with hundreds of unique pictures. Obviously, blond Jesus in a bathrobe made an appearance. Jesus with children on his knee against a backdrop of frolicking lambs was also common. There was Jamaican dreadlock Rasta Jesus, Icon with a halo glow Jesus, goalie Jesus saving a shot (Jesus saves!), and bodybuilding Jesus showing off his guns (His pain, your gain!). There was beauty and nonsense. It became obvious to all of us that we've created Jesus in our own image.

This assignment was also personal. A tour to Israel in the year 2000, as I look back now, changed my life forever. Before that trip, I had no plans to study the Bible, no plans to teach high school, and no plans to lead a megachurch. The land, the text, the history, and the culture totally surprised me. But so did my own questions. I started asking, for the first time in my life, "Who was the real Jesus?" And this launched a new wandering, through new books, and new cities, and new voices, many from the theological fringe. I read everything I could on the historical Jesus. I went to graduate school because of this unanswerable question.

Though the real Jesus never really emerged, a new shadow danced upon the wall. I could almost make out the image of a man of his own era, inside his own nuanced religion, speaking his own language. To my relief, he had almost nothing to do with the blond guy in a bathrobe. And for me, and also for my students, to bring Jesus out of the clouds and back to earth made Christianity a little less like a fairy tale and more of a tangible adventure. A real man, from a real place, walking on the actual earth, doing ordinary stuff was a great relief to us all.

And this idea really changed me: Jesus's self-identifying title was "Son of Man," *ben adam*, a way of identifying with our shared humanity. Jesus was saying, "I am the human one." This title alone is a clue that Jesus seems more interested in being human than being a God.

Christianity has been overly concerned with the divinity of Jesus. The early church basically adopted Roman / notions of imperial divinity and placed them on the Son of Man. It was a way of saying, "Our divine king is the real divine king, not Caesar," which was politically brave and noble. But we lost our way in all this divinity business. We even let imperial notions of victory, warfare, and domination form the foundation of our future hopes. We basically want Jesus to return as a super-human-divine warrior and kick ass. We really want Caesar, not a peasant-rabbi. But returning to a more historical Jesus sobers us up from our imperial pipedreams about a future empire where there will "more with us than there will be with them."

What I discovered as I shed a few more pounds from my camel is that Jesus came to teach us what it means to be human, not to announce his divinity. He even tells most people who call him the "Son of God" to be quiet. Our shared humanity is what makes Jesus's teachings worth paying attention to. He shared our experience, in its totality, from suffering to ecstasy. He didn't come to take us away from our humanity, or away from the earth, but more deeply into those things. This is the real genius of Christianity.

When we move into our deepest human nature, we find God, the divine source of everything. The incarnation, the word becoming flesh, also happens in us. We too are divine words being made flesh in our time and place. This is actually an orthodox teaching in the church.[3] Our true humanity is the discovery that we are also sons and daughters of God, all divine words, spoken into being. A healthier spirituality for the next century is one in which we move more into our raw humanity and not pine to escape the complexity of just being human.

I used to lie in bed at night, afraid to go to sleep. The morning might mean the rapture had already happened and I'd been left behind. I imagined that I'd wake to find empty beds with my parents' clothes crumpled on the sheets. They'd all be in heaven, and I'd be stuck on earth where all hell would break lose.

But the word *rapture* is a mistranslation from the Greek, to the Latin, and into the King James. So much fear and anxiety over a mistranslation! Paul was actually using the imagery and language that Caesar used when he appeared outside any Roman city for a visit, or when he returned to Rome from a battle.[4] The entire city was "caught up" in this "appearance," rushed out to great him, and welcomed him

---

3. This is known as *theosis* or deification in the Orthodox Church. See Timothy Ware, *The Orthodox Church* (London: Penguin, 1993), 231–38.

into the city for a visit. This was called the *Parousia*, meaning *presence* or *appearance*.

To be *caught* or *seized* by the appearance of Christ is really what Paul's image conveys. The church is caught up in an entirely anti-imperial image of a true savior. For Paul, this appearance, where we are seized by a whole new image of the divine, degraded Caesar's appearance in the empire. No wonder Caesar had Paul executed.

I don't think the question for the future is about when the physical Jesus will appear in the sky and take us all away. The question is on the mystical level. We're being invited to welcome the cosmic Christ into the city *right now*. We're being asked to live a life animated by the divine presence of Christ, being born in the human soul, right now. We're being asked to put our hope in a mysterious indwelling rather than temporal powers, egotistical rulers like Caesar, and tribal notions of safety, security, and salvation for just a few citizens.

For many centuries, we've imagined that Jesus's second coming was going to clean up the mess he couldn't fix the first time. Christians took the messianic expectations of a physical king, which Jesus rejected, and projected them onto the future.

We don't need Jesus to come back. He's already here.

Jesus isn't up in heaven making us a sweet suburban house, biding his time till he feels like coming again and plucking the faithful off of the doomed earth, only to give

---

4. See my discussion and sources in *NIV First-Century Study Bible* (Grand Rapids: Zondervan, 2014), 1529.

us a better one after destroying it. Any verse in the Bible or teaching of the church that hints at these things is symbolic. Paul's image of the living body of Christ is all the second coming we need: "Now you are the body of Christ, each one of you is a part of it" (1 Corinthians 12:27). Maybe taking this verse more literally and the "rapture" stuff less so would help. The living body of Christ is already present. And this body is totally diverse; all the parts matter—the hands and feet, the languages and expressions that make up this mystical whole.

Listen to Jesus's most provocative words: "One day you will realize that I am in the Father, and you are in me, and I am in you." This is the real second coming. This is the coming of the cosmic and mystical Christ. This is Christ consciousness. This is the shift to new ways of thinking and being in the world. It's like we're born again. It's like being caught up in the clouds with Christ. It's like the Spirit of God welling up from within like living water.

The first verse I learned in Sunday school was, "For God so loved the world." And soon I learned another: "God is love" (1 John 4:8). If only we could come to live as if this were true. Such a vision of love transforms our relationship with everything that's real.

The ground we tread upon is holy ground, and it always has been. Everything is sacred, and the divine words are everywhere. God is just fine with our naked humanity, for God is in that too. The dawn of this way of being in the world is the second coming of Christ.

7

AVOID GETTING SAVED

The two strongest memories of my childhood are the oaks behind the house and the sprawling buildings, stages, and pews of Thomas Road Baptist Church. I used to play in the green rooms and sound studios behind the massive stage in that church. I spent Wednesday night, Sunday morning, and Sunday night in church. I went to Sunday school and worshiped in the sanctuary. During the week I went to Jerry Falwell's elementary school, which was on the same campus as the church. The sole purpose of all this churchgoing was to get saved and to make sure others were saved. I heard a lot about the "plan of salvation."

But there's something funny about the evangelical pre-occupation with getting saved. Here's Jesus on the matter: "Anyone who wants to save his life will lose it."

From where I stand now, it looks like the church of my youth got it backwards. Making every effort to secure our home in heaven by saying the magic words, or belonging to just the right tribe, or believing just the right things, or being baptized with the right water at the right age (Adult baptism! we argued), ended up taking up all our religious energy. We've fulfilled Jesus's words, by losing any sense of what's important in life.

An Israeli friend once asked me why Christians keep asking him if he's saved. He was genuinely puzzled. I started to explain to him the plan of salvation, being a sinner, believing in Jesus, the whole lot. He interrupted, "I already know all that. I know what you all believe about Jesus covering all your sins, going to heaven and everything, that's not what I mean. I want to know why it's in the past tense."

"Seriously?" I wondered out loud.

"It doesn't make any sense to me," he continued. "How can anyone get 'saved,' some time in the past? I mean, shouldn't Jesus be 'saving' us, in the present tense? Do you really think God did something once, when you first believed in Jesus?"

I tried to clear things up. "This kind of salvation is about believing something specific, a few words, at some point in the past, and then you're 'saved.' And if you believe these things, then you're good to go. They just want you to believe in Jesus so you won't burn in hell. They call this 'getting saved.'"

"That's ridiculous," he said. "I live my life as a Jew. I try to love God in my own way. And I hope that God is saving me, right now. But it's never over. No one is 'saved.' There is no special belief that gives you the kind of life I'm talking about."

And that's just it. Out of the mouth of the "unsaved": salvation.

Continuing to grow into a life of wholeness, beauty, compassion, presence, grace, and love is what I now call *salvation*. Participating in making our world, our cultures and societies, a little more whole, sounds like salvation. Worrying about my eternal address or being in the right group is hell.

Part of the reason we got so hung up on our incomplete notions of salvation is because we thought that Jesus did something *for* us. We thought that a long time ago it all happened, and if we just believed it, in our heads, then what was done *for* us would be credited to our account before God. This transactional view of salvation dominated my own thinking. Jesus was the mechanism by which God accepted my wretchedness. He was the right coin to drop in the salvation machine, as long as I had the correct beliefs.

For evangelicals in particular, we also believed quite literally that the blood of Jesus atoned for our sins, as if physical blood was necessary for this transactional formula to work. We accidentally literalized the ancient sacrificial system, as if God needed blood to accept us. In this way of thinking, Jesus suffered *for* us, and his blood covers our unworthiness. Jesus got what we deserved.

But a bloodthirsty God who needs to torture his son just so he can accept us isn't very good news. A healthy spirituality, even a healthy Christianity, must walk out on transactional atonement. It's an unhelpful and damaging view of

God based on a degraded view that human beings are essentially worthless.

Salvation is about a certain way of being and becoming in the world. There's no magic formula that gets you across the line. Just because you convert to Christianity doesn't mean you're living a life of salvation. Salvation is a metaphor for a life lived with greater and greater integration and wholeness. In fact, the "saving" I'm trying to describe has very little to do with what religion we belong to.

Don't Convert

When I first became interested in Judaism, before I moved to Israel, the rabbi at my local synagogue in Michigan allowed my dad and me to take his conversion class, with one stipulation: we couldn't convert. I'd never heard of a religion that was reluctant for converts. We learned that Judaism actually turns away prospective converts three times before even starting the conversation about joining. Unlike my Christian view of conversion, we spent the entire class talking about how to live as Jews rather than what to believe. It seemed like I could almost convert to Judaism without any profession of faith or public declaration of belief (though circumcision was required—ouch). This wasn't a religion I recognized.

To be frank, I really wanted to convert to Judaism. The notion of leaving one thing and moving into something else drew me. I wanted a change, and I wanted *to* change. But as the class went on, the very word *conversion* became less

clear. How does one leave one worldview and enter another? \
When is it clear that one belief system has replaced another?
And even if I swapped out all my Christian beliefs for Jewish ones, had I really changed, or was I simply exchanging
my group for one I found more appealing?

I have the sense that to leave home for something else
is more like falling in love than graduating with a diploma.
You know you're in love when you're in love, but it's hard
to say precisely when the love started, when you actually
found yourself in love.

When we locate our moment of salvation—our conversion—in the past, marked by a special prayer or holy water,
we rob ourselves of the anticipation and recognition of the
ongoing work of Mystery happening in the soul. We can
say, "Something shifted back then," or "Something was
rearranged," but we cannot declare a definitive moment of
conversion.

We also tend to think that when we believe something,
or say we believe something, that it actually changes how we
live. But this is rarely the case. As Richard Rohr writes, "We
cannot think into new ways of living, we must live into new
ways of thinking."[1] Real conversion is about living into new
ways of being. Over time, like falling in love, we might be
able to say, "Hey wait, I no longer think the way I used to. I
know this because I am no longer living the way I used to. I
am being converted. In my own small way, I am living a new
life that tastes a little more like salvation."

1. Richard Rohr, *Everything Belongs: The Gift of Contemplative Prayer* (New York: Crossroad, 2003).

A few years after my conversion class, I had moved to Israel, still pursuing a big change in my life, still wondering if I might need to convert to something. If not Judaism, maybe I needed some mystical and ancient expression of Christianity. I took a course on Eastern Orthodox liturgy taught by a Lutheran minister and professor, Petra Heldt. A suicide bomber in the main Jerusalem market had injured her in the 1990s, and her face bore the scars. I loved her fierce passion for all things old. We took extensive field trips to monasteries and followed the seminarian monks as they sang the Armenian liturgy in the Church of the Holy Sepulcher. I asked her once, after trying to follow the liturgy for about half-an-hour, if we were nearing the end. She said, "That was one verse, of one song."

One day I asked her why she didn't just convert to Orthodoxy. She smiled and said, "Oh, I don't believe in conversion." I felt a little embarrassed because I'd spent so much of my time thinking about converting, whether it be Judaism, or some unfamiliar Christian tradition, as long as it was old.

After a minute of playing it cool, like I agreed with her, I said, "Why not? You seem to love all this stuff more than your own tradition."

Then she said something that surprised me: "I don't believe in conversion because I don't think God wants anyone to leave his or her own tradition. Each one is unique. The Orthodox Church and the ancient liturgies from around the world only make me a better Lutheran. When I stand up in my own church on Sunday morning, I can hear their voices ringing in my ears. The truth is, I'm richer because of it. Studying all these things only changes me for the better."

And that's what I wanted too, to be changed for the better. When I walked out of class that day, I felt the weight of my own quest had lightened a bit. Maybe it wasn't about converting *to* something, but being converted *by* something. Maybe it wasn't about adding layers, even really old ones, but taking layers off the camel—allowing myself to be changed by something.

The Bible tells us that Paul got knocked down and blinded by the Risen Christ on the road to Damascus. This is often called his "conversion." But according to the story, he was blinded for three days and was led by the hand. He wasn't able to control much of anything, an important symbol for what real change looks like. Stumbling around in the dark is at least as important as the flashes of light. Paul encountered a mystery, but only later did he put language around it. And to be fair, the story of this encounter isn't even written by Paul but by his friend Luke, in the book of Acts.

After this dramatic encounter, Paul went to see Peter to chat about his experience, about three years later. Apparently Paul spent these years in the Arabian Desert, but he doesn't say what he was doing. Trying to cope? Trying to hide? Wandering around? Asking God what the hell was happening? Paul finally starts to travel around the empire, telling people about his experience—fifteen years later! Only after a decade-and-a-half is he ready to talk about all that's been happening in his life. When did it start? It doesn't matter. When did he convert? Who can say?! But enough time passed for him to live into a new way of thinking.

Some of the academic literature on conversion claims that learning how to talk about one's conversion is a big part of the conversion experience. The skeptic says that we convert to a way of speaking about conversion. I know this from my own evangelical past, because we had to learn how to talk about getting saved in order to be in the saved group. But this isn't what happened to Paul. He wasn't concerned about conformity. He used his own language, in his own way. And he remained a radical outsider, even to the inner circle of Jesus followers, until his untimely death.

In Paul, it's a transformation, not a conversion, of living, being, consciousness, ideas, thoughts, and actions. It happens over time. It happens slowly. It happens inconsistently at first, more lived than believed. It might contain a flash of blinding light, but then it's three days of darkness, and many years of slowly allowing this reality to grow. The juxtapositions between insight and confusion, darkness and light, previous beliefs and new experiences, are simply a part of transformation's work.

This matters because our expectations need to change about the nature of spiritual growth and transformation. The process is slow. Teilhard de Chardin wrote,

Above all, trust in the slow work of God. We are quite naturally impatient to reach the end without delay. We should like

116

*to skip the intermediate stages. We are impatient of being on
the way to something unknown, something new. And yet it is
the law of all progress that it is made by passing through some
stage of instability—and that it might take a very long time.*[2]

We're on the way to a transformed life, a destination at
which we will never arrive. Our groping in the darkness is
as much a part of the slow work of change as the blinding
light of a passing moment. Transformation holds the para-
doxes of gift and action, prayer and letting go, desire and
frustration, darkness and light. And to be transformed like
this propels us forward, into another room, to the edge of
another liminal threshold, toward another country of
greater wholeness and wonder. We shed more than we gain,
at least at first. And if we're to learn anything from our own
saints and mystics, the more transformation that's taking
place, the further we seem to be from the mainstream of religious thought and practice. This really shouldn't surprise
us. Jesus doesn't fit neatly into any expression of first-century Judaism that we know of, nor of any Christian tradition
born in his name.

GIVING UP SALVATION

Jesus says quite plainly, "Anyone who would come after
me must deny himself, take up his cross, and follow" (Matt
16:24). This verse has always bothered me, for it's often used
to put our passions and desires down, to crush our dreams

2. See Michael J. Harter, S.J., *Heart on Fire* (Chicago: Loyola, 2005).

and hopes. But I don't think that's what Jesus was talking about. He was talking about the unique path that only we can walk, the burden that only we can carry.

In other words, Jesus cannot carry our cross. He can't do it for us. He carried his own cross, in his own time and place, but each of us must carry our own: uniqueness, present circumstances, histories and hang-ups, roles and stories, traumas and grief, love affairs and heartbreaks, longings and desires. We carry these to a hill on which they die and are reborn. They don't go away, they're transformed. And on the way, we deny the first journey, our first persona, our first ego, our false self, to discover a deeper and truer self. We're being born again.

One of the most important things we can do right now is give up on being saved. We might even need to give up on identifying as a Christian. My tradition promised assurance of our salvation if we believed the right things. What I moved into as I passed further through the eye of the needle was the absence of such assurance. Our obsession with these things has kept our own egos firmly in charge. By clinging tightly to being in the saved camp, our lives often remain unchanged and stagnant. I'm not pointing the finger; it's been true in my own life. I may have claimed to be "saved," but that doesn't mean I was living a life of radical love, inclusion, grace, mercy, forgiveness, humility, openness, and wonder.

The Pascal Mystery is the ancient name for the story of Jesus's life, particularly his final days in Jerusalem. The name describes the mystery of death and resurrection. The early

Christians had the insight to call the whole story a mystery in the first place, but it wasn't just about what happened to Jesus. They called it the Pascal Mystery because they saw within it a greater pattern of truth. What's true about Jesus's life, death, and resurrection is a pattern of truth, and it's available to all people.

It's a truth we undergo. Because truth happens *in* us, not *for* us.

It doesn't matter what literally happened to Jesus, at least not in the way we've been taught. What matters is what's happening in us. This sounds like heresy, but it's not. The Enlightenment categories that pigeonholed truth into the objective and historical were short-sighted. Thankfully the changes in cultural thought about the nature of truth have pulled the rug out from such idolatry.

This way of looking at things changed my own faith. I started to realize that if I were going to understand Jesus in an authentic way, I was going to have to drop most of the doctrinal wrestling matches, my beliefs, and my technical arguments about theology, and pay attention to what was happening in my own heart. When we give up on being saved we actually fall more easily into our undoing, which is precisely the point.

I had to take responsibility for who I was, as best I could, and walk toward the hill of my death and resurrection. Not that I could manufacture this descent and ascent. I could only say "yes" and move toward the edge. Some of this occurred to me in the middle of a sermon. I remember thinking one Sunday morning, as I looked out at the familiar faces, many of whose names I didn't even know, that if I hadn't experienced what I was talking about, I ought not to be talking about it. The problem was, this left me with very little to say, except maybe that I was unsure of a lot of what passed as religious truth. I heard Richard Rohr's observation ringing in my head, instead of focusing on my sermon, "You can only take people as far as you yourself have gone."[3] I wanted to go further, but being some kind of spiritual expert held me back.

Unfortunately, spiritual leadership is too often about having the right answers for every situation or theological question—the better the leader, the quicker and clearer the answers. But I had to stop playing this game. I had to admit that I didn't know what I was talking about, and walk toward my own undoing. In other words, it was time to take up my own particular cross and edge closer to my own spiritual death.

Jesus says, "Unless a grain of wheat falls to the ground and dies it remains a single seed. But if the grain of wheat dies and goes into the ground, it reaps ten, twenty, even a hundred times" (John 12:24). A lot of contemporary Christianity is a seed unplanted, a grain of wheat on the shelf, a set of abstract beliefs and "objective" truths, untested and unknown but waiting to go into the ground of transformation.

The priest and author Ronald Rolheiser writes, "The Pascal Mystery is the mystery of how we, after undergoing

---

3. I heard Richard Rohr say this at a conference in New Mexico.

some kind of death, receive new life and new spirit. Jesus, in both his teaching and his life, showed us a clear paradigm for how this should happen."[4]

In fact, all the stories, poems, and literary jewels of the Bible contain patterns that are true. The stories point beyond themselves to truths that happen in us, in our hearts and in our communities. The patterns are spiritually true, which is another way of saying actually true.

Like Abraham we leave home.

Like Jacob we wrestle with God.

Like Sarah we are barren.

Like Joseph we are betrayed.

Like David we sleep with our neighbor and cover it up.

Like Ruth we realize we're God's daughter, even though biblical religion has left us out.

Like Isaiah we have a vision of Reality that sears our lips.

Like Samson we're blinded by our own lust.

Like Elijah we find God in a whisper rather than a storm.

Like Jonah we run from God, only to be swallowed whole.

Like Jesus, we die and are resurrected.

So here are the important questions in my mind these days: Where are we in the story, in the Pascal Mystery, in the pattern of death and resurrection? Can we find a bit of ourselves in the grand narrative staring back at us? The answers are hard. There's confusion, hope, betrayal, denial, abandonment, false accusations, public shame, forsakenness,

---

4. Ronald Rolheiser, *The Holy Longing: The Search for a Christian Spirituality* (New York: Doubleday, 1999), 145.

rumors of new life, and encounters with resurrected figures. And these are just a few of the realities that happened in the last week of Jesus's life!

If we can say yes, that some of these things are happening in us, then we're living into the Pascal Mystery. The story is happening in the deepest recesses of our being. It's true because it's happening, not because it happened. Our plans, dreams, marriages, partnerships, friendships, careers, failures, theologies, beliefs, moments of conversion, our ideas about church, all die and are reborn. But this requires serious letting go in order to follow in the way of Jesus's pattern.

The camel has to be naked to pass through the gate.

8

THE WALL OF A
KNOWABLE GOD

Once I used a line from Thomas Merton in a sermon: "People can spend all their time climbing the ladder of success only to find, after reaching the top, the ladder is leaning against the wrong wall."[1] I even climbed a ladder on stage to make the point. I stood up there, making everyone nervous, thinking I was pretty clever. But it would've been a more honest illustration if I had fallen off. Merton was talking about the spiritual life more than the corner office of business success.

And I thought I was speaking to the congregation. But I realized that I was on the ladder. And I was on the wrong wall. I was standing up there alone, wondering how I ever got here. I'd been dispensing spiritual talks instead of living my own questions. I looked around and had no one left to

---

1. See the introduction to Richard Rohr, *Falling Upward: A Spirituality for the Two Halves of Life* (San Francisco: Jossey-Bass, 2011), xvii.

blame but myself. I'd climbed the ladder while quoting lines about climbing the ladder.

I no longer felt satisfied just talking about spiritual stuff or pointing to a book, saying the truth is over there. I couldn't just keep quoting authors I liked or saying I believed something when I didn't. I couldn't keep asking other voices in my life what to do or trying to please various loyal soldiers. Probably like a lot of spiritual teachers, talking about spirituality had become a substitute for my own spiritual life. A few more items had to come off the camel's back. Otherwise, I was just going to keep repeating myself to death. One day, I had to come down, even if it killed me. I had to save my own life by coming down off the wall.

I wasn't a spiritual expert, or God's messenger, or the spiritual answer man, or Moses wielding the divine word of God. I wanted a new kind of inner knowing, or unknowing, born out of authenticity, experience, and humility. It didn't matter any more if it conformed to the religious categories I'd known and preached about. The wall I'd been climbing since childhood knew all about God and was pretty sure of itself. But inside my heart, I wasn't sure if I knew anything about this God anymore. All my great sermons full of many words seemed to be getting in the way. Yet I had a curious feeling that something dormant just woke up.

THE KNOWLEDGE OF UNKNOWING

I wonder what it really means that the God of the ancient Hebrews couldn't be carved in stone or wood. One on level, an image gives the worshiper a kind of false certainty; we're pretty sure we know what we're looking at. But there's a deep truth behind the first of the Ten Commandments, "Make no graven image," even if we have as hard a time keeping this commandment as did ancient Israel. This way of un-imagining God was unlike any of the other cultures from that time period. The Bible is saying that no visual image of God is needed. The closest the Bible comes to images is in its poetry, where God is merely *like* a stone, or a whirlwind, or a shepherd, or a desert stream, or a mother hen, or the sound of sheer silence.

Shortly before the time of Jesus, a legend surfaced that the Roman General Pompey went behind the sacred curtain of the Temple in Jerusalem when Rome swept the Greek empire, and he found only an empty room. This is a powerful symbol of where the divine quest may actually be leading us: to emptiness.

There's nothing inherently wrong with comparing God to this or that. We don't have any other tools at our disposal, and it seems to be a natural part of our growing in faith. To say God is like a father is not a bad way to start. But God is only *like* a father. Our images only take us so far. It's wildly freeing to say every image of God falls short. It's generous and life-giving to realize that every idea of God fails to sum up God.

I had lunch with a pastor in my hometown not that long ago. The conversation turned toward how we study for sermons and make decisions. He told me, in no uncertain terms, that God tells him what to preach on, what to say, and what to do through his prayers. God tells him how to interpret scripture and what leaders to hire or fire. I sat there dumbfounded, not knowing how to respond. This was miles from my own experience. The certainty with which he talked about God didn't ring true to me.

A God who goes around telling people what to do, what to say, what to preach on, who to fire, when to build a new building, that was the sky-God who kept unraveling for me. A God who already has everything jotted down in his massive day-planner and is waiting for me to figure it out wasn't compelling anymore. I didn't believe in that God anymore. The feeling I had was, "I'm trying to listen, I'm trying to pay attention, but I'm unsure about this whole God business."

It seems like now even the word *God* isn't working. At its worst, that word is another golden calf. Our certainty about this God is an idol, a substitute for the real thing. It's an image that we're bowing down before, an image we can control and promote, a God who does things the way we think they should be done, votes the way we vote, sees the world the way we see it. The word *God*, and our certainty about that God and that word, is blocking us from the Mystery that is God.

That's what I realized and what I preached in my resignation sermon: we don't know what we mean by *God* anymore.

SITTING IN THE UNKNOWING

This is a gift and an invitation. We need to hang out here for a while. We need to get to know our unknowing. We need to lie down in the lawn on clear night like Isaiah did and wonder, "Who created all this?" But then not answer the question. The question needs to work on us. Because there are some questions that aren't worth answering. They're worth living.

When I told my congregation that it was time for me to step aside, I talked a bit about moving toward the edge of faith. I said that I'd always been drawn away from the center. In fact, I was no longer interested in defending or promoting what passed as the center of the Christian faith. I was unsure of the word *God*.

"We don't know what we mean by God anymore." Although I had said that in previous sermons, this line turned out to be revealing, and people heard it quite differently on the Sunday that I resigned. Many people in the congregation really resonated with what I was trying to describe, for they felt the same way. But for others, it was the reason I had to go, for it was evidence of my unbelief. And they were right. I was an unbeliever. But this kind of unbelief is a necessary part of getting to a naked camel.

Every spoken word and every image of God is just an approximation. This isn't New Ageism. Something like this could be the first line in every statement of faith, creed, or doctrinal decree. A new creed might sound like this:

We bear witness to the mystery of existence, to Reality, to our best attempts at naming the Divine, who is beyond all our striving. We honor the mystery of being alive as pure gift. We trust that whatever we mean by God—is just a hint. And we trust that this hint is loving and is love.

This is the mystical tradition of orthodox Christianity, particularly the Christianity of the deserts and back alleys. By orthodox, I mean it the old-fashioned way, "straight praise," which is what the word actually means. Being orthodox isn't about having the right beliefs, words, or doctrines. It's about uttering words of praise to the Mystery—nothing more and nothing less. Saying, "I don't know" is orthodox. Asking, "Who created all this?" is orthodox.

I'm not against the old doctrines. Many of them are songs of mystery, poems of praise to the unknown God. Has anyone ever explained the Trinity and sounded like they were making perfect sense? It's a poem! Or the virgin birth, which is an image of the mysterious divine indwelling, the openness to receiving this mystery. Has fully-man-and-fully-God ever sounded rational? It's a work of art. We gaze upon it rather than explain it, defend it, or weaponize it.

Orthodox truths are songs, poems, approximations, paintings, ruminations, and prayers. They're transparent images that we gaze through to something beyond, like a stained-glass window. If we can say it differently now, with new images, inspired by the old, so be it. It's one grand and beautiful conversation anyway.

This requires a certain kind of inner posture toward the divine, the unknown, the Mystery. It's a letting go of what we've known up to this point. It's scary. It feels wrong. Some loyal part of ourselves warns us to run back home, to climb back up the ladder, to stick to the old-time religion. But we can't. Instead we must set off toward the hidden Mystery, which is what the saints and mystics and heretics did. So we're not alone.

THE APOPHATIC PATH

As should be clear by now, when I first moved to Israel I was obsessed with Judaism—like dating a girl my parents didn't approve of. But the longer I stayed, the more I became intrigued by my own Christian tradition. I realized how little I knew about the history of my own faith, and I had to admit that my own evangelical slice of Christianity was one tiny offshoot of a tree that went back thousands of years. My version of Christianity would've been unrecognizable to most Christians who have ever lived, not to mention Jesus.

So I explored Eastern Christianity and the mystical tradition. I read texts that I had no idea existed. I heard ways of speaking about God that sounded like a foreign language. I thought, "If I talked like this in church, I would be called a heretic." They did things with scripture that would result in a failing grade in the college Bible classes I took. I wondered what God many of these writers were even speaking about. I heard a whole new way of honoring the mystery of

life, and the mystery of God. I discovered, almost by acci-
dent, the apophatic tradition.

The *kataphatic* tradition speaks of God in the positive. It
speaks in images and words. It's what we in the West were
raised on: "God is like . . . God is. . . ."

The *apophatic* tradition speaks of God in the negative,
about what God is not, or by subtraction. It speaks without
images and without words. God is wordless. God cannot be
spoken about. God has no name. God has no form. God has
no image. God is not an object. God is not a being, as we
understand a being. God doesn't even exist, at least in the
way we understand existence. We cannot say anything at all
about God, because no language is adequate. In fact, we cannot think anything at all about God, because God cannot be
thought of and is beyond thought.

I couldn't believe this was inside the Orthodox (and
orthodox!) tradition. Christianity was far richer than I ever
gave it credit for; you just have to turn off the cable channels
and the radio, close most of the books in the Christian
bookstore, and stop going to church to hear it. All these
intuitions of mine, that God couldn't be like this or that,
turned out to be inside my own religion! They turned out to
be holy, not profane.

At the heart of this kind of Christianity is a living paradox: we can know God, yet we cannot know God. As
Thomas Aquinas says, "The extreme of human knowledge
of God is to know that we do not know God."[2] This kind of

2. Quoted by Thomas Moore in the introduction to Thomas Merton, *Conjectures
of a Guilty Bystander* (New York: Image/Doubleday, 2009).

mystical spirituality is Christianity at its most mature. And we all have some growing up to do. We barely hear anybody speak with this kind of wisdom anymore.

This sort of tension and paradox rang my bell. Something deep inside me said, "You can trust this. Go as far as you can, even if you don't know where you're going."

Not that I turned into some kind of mystic. Anyone who claims to be a mystic probably isn't. A mystic is one who's had an experience of the transcendent, the mystery, the nameless one, God. Maybe they talk about it, but most likely they don't. If they do talk about it, it will probably sound a bit like heresy. For example, Paul claims that he visited a "third heaven," but then he refuses to describe the experience. If Paul were around today we'd demand proof for his outrageous claims and then dismiss him when he refused. The mystical path is quiet. It's lived mostly without words.

Walking near the gates of the apophatic tradition softened the walls around my own heart. And then the sisters at the Dominican Center back in Michigan taught me to pay attention to my own life, however small and subtle. They claimed that an experience of God is there, hidden and not hidden, for those who have eyes to see. They had more faith that the mystery of God was present in my own life than I did, whether or not I "believed" in God.

My hang-ups with evangelicalism, which needed some airing out and some post-traumatic recovery, could've easily become a block if I stayed there very long. It's possible for people like me to spend our whole lives complaining or fighting the small tradition we inherited. But encountering a contemplative and mystical expression of faith gave me a glimpse of a new country I'd only dreamed about. I wanted to visit this place—maybe I already had, the sisters kept insisting. And this new country was inhabited by some Christians, and by other traditions as well, and by a few with no recognizable tradition at all!

UNKNOWING GOD

Whatever our starting place with God, it's only a starting place. Whatever we've been told about God, for good or bad, is the opening chapter. My hope is that it's truly a starting place. My prayer is that it's a beginning, not a block. At some point we come down off the ladder of our initial ideas of faith.

No church, no writer, no Bible verse, no saint, no preacher, no religion, no denomination, no image, no doctrine, sums up the Mystery. If you have serious doubts about God, great. You may just be at the edge of a cliff, but it's not a cliff into God-less-ness. To jump is to begin a deeper faith story. All the saints and mystics insist that to jump—or more likely to fall—is to be held in a darkness of Love. It's to be in a cloud of unknowing, which is a cloud of love. In fact, the author of the classic mystical text *The Cloud of Unknowing* calls the first step a "cloud of forgetfulness." We must forget what we've learned about God if we're to go any further. This was completely counterintuitive to my own Western Christian ideas of growing in the "knowledge of God."

Unknowing is part of faith. Unlearning is part of grow-

132

ing up. Letting go of what once worked is holy. Some of our long-held images of God have to go, be forgotten, set down in order to lighten the load. Some of them may come back, some will not. This unknowing doesn't cling to any image of God; it transcends our original images, whether they were healthy or unhealthy.

We're able to say, "Yes, God is a Father, and that's okay," even if God is equally a Mother, or is both genders, or beyond gender. We can see that these early images were pointing beyond themselves. They were rest stops on the way to something bigger. Looking at the Bible in all its messiness, we're able to see patterns of deeper truth all along, between the words so to speak. Let's not forget that God didn't give Moses an answer about the true nature of his name more than 3,000 years ago. God said, "I will be, what I will be." Knowing and unknowing are hidden in the Bible in plain sight.

The most important thing I could do is to get really honest about my own experience. It's not as easy as it sounds to forget about the preachers, or our parents, or our spouse, or all the spiritual advice we've consumed. What is my rock-bottom experience of God, whether I think I have one or not?

The edge of faith is a time to get honest about our actual living theology, not the one we profess. Our real hopes and questions, the ones we have a hard time even looking at, need some air. I think it's important to ask, if there were no judges, if we didn't have to get the words right: what, or who, is God to us, right now. The truth is, for all of us, our early images and ideas of God are inside a leaky container, and the contents are spilling out. Let's not work so hard to clean up the mess, at least not right away.

"Do not be afraid," is the number one expression in the Bible when people have divine encounters, so let's not worry. God is with us and in us already. It's an amazing time to be alive. We're at the edge of unknowing what's already known. We're stepping toward something we cannot grasp in the ways we've always grasped. We're passing through the eye of the needle once again.

Scholars talk about this type of space as liminal, threshold space. We've left one room and not quite entered another. We've let go of certain early images of God, but haven't seen the fullness of something else. We've come down the ladder, but we're not sure what direction to walk. Our authority systems have cracked, and the new authority of our own experience is just arriving. But liminal space is where real change happens, even though it's scary and sometimes hurts. We might have to wrestle all night in the dark like Jacob, only to walk away free but with a limp.

SWALLOWED LIKE JONAH

Apparently, the people who followed Jesus asked him for a sign, proof that he was the promised Messiah, or at least a prophet sent by God. I know how they felt. I've looked for a lot of signs in my life. That's part of the reason I climbed Sinai. Even when I was a kid I asked God to turn the lights off in church, just for one second, so that I could know he was real. I wondered sometimes if he really did turn off the lights, while I blinked, but I'd missed it. It's pretty natural to look for proof of the things we've been told about, but Jesus doesn't play the proof game.

Jesus said, "No sign shall be given to you but the sign of Jonah. Just as Jonah spent three days and three nights in the belly of a fish, so the Son of Man will spend three days and three nights in the heart of the earth" (Luke 11:29).

The easy explanation for this enigmatic line is to say that Jesus is foreshadowing his own death and resurrection, but this only scratches the surface. Whatever Jesus is saying about himself, he's also saying to us. We too must spend three days and three nights in the belly of the fish, the center of darkness, and the heart of the earth.

To be fully human is to follow the pattern Jesus is talking about. To wake up to the fullness of our own lives here on earth, in the kingdom of the nameless one, requires something of our own descent, burial, and return. The sign of Jonah is the image of our own death and resurrection, as it was for Jesus. And here is where things get interesting. The pattern of Jonah is pretty clear.

1. He hears a call, a call to something deeper, a mission and destiny.
2. He runs from God and from this destiny.
3. He's caught anyway, swallowed by death, and he descends into darkness for three days.
4. Then he's spit out on the shore and walks toward his destiny.

5. He fulfills his calling, though reluctantly, and with some doubts.

6. Finally, he's angry that God has mercy on his enemies, is shown how little he knows about the mysterious ways of God, and the story ends with a question from God, "Should I not have concern for the great city of Nineveh, in which there are more than a hundred and twenty thousand people who cannot tell their right hand from their left—and also many animals?"

Jonah and the fish isn't a cute kid's story. It's disturbing, funny, absurd, satirical, and a little difficult to be certain of the story's point. It leaves us with more questions than answers. Will Jonah remain stuck in his small way of thinking, or will his ideas and experience of God expand? Will something of his old life die and be reborn? Who is this God? A tribal deity or the God of the people of Nineveh as well? The story ends without clear answers, because it's not about answers, it's about the pattern of Jonah's life. You won't see many self-help spiritual books using the arc of Jonah's life because so much popular spirituality is about shoring up our small selves and never dying into something larger.

What's missing in a lot of contemporary Christianity, or even spirituality more broadly, is that we never get going on the sacred pattern of descent that Jesus says is our sign. We never run from God. We never argue back. We never let our original ideas of God fail us. We never step out.

Instead we talk ourselves out of the mysterious call that's whispering in the backrooms of our soul. And the lack of willingness to run, or leave, or resist, means we have no access to the rest of the story. We cannot pass through the belly of the fish because we don't want to take the first step.

RUN LIKE HELL

Like the hero's journey in the archetypal stories of human-ity, the first step is the hardest. The first step is to leave home. For many of us, leaving home means leaving the church. We must break our parents' hearts and run. Many of us have to give the finger to the well-intentioned pastor and head for the exits, break with the conversation at the Thanksgiving table or we'll never grow up. We have to say, "I can no longer accept the God of my childhood and my church and the cliché platitudes that pass as spirituality."

If we don't learn to run, we'll never know that the truth we are seeking happens in us and to us, in the patterns, images, stories, and experiences of our own lives. If we don't get on the boat and push out into the unknown we never descend to discover deeper gifts that we are to bring back to our people. The pattern is to run, be shoved overboard, swallowed, receive new gifts in the belly of the whale, and return to serve a larger vision.

What I'm arguing for requires radical authenticity all along this second journey. Attempting to fit in, to placate, to go numb, to play some game, keeps us from leaving home, and thus from undergoing the transformational pattern of Jonah. Had he said, "Alright God, no problem, I'll be a good little prophet," there would be no story. And the church is full of people, even leaders, who've never left home. This means they've not gone through the very pattern that Jesus says is absolutely essential and is our sign.

But here's where we learn a new kind of faith, one that isn't based on abstract theological beliefs or statements. We learn to trust, by our own staggering experience of descent and death, that the mystery of God is cooperating with our running, resisting, questioning, fleeing, doubting, depression, addiction, hoping, loving, leaving, and returning. Through this descent we discover the great secret of real spiritual transformation: to go down is the path to a greater going up, to union and to wholeness. In the sweet darkness of the whale's belly we get a glimpse of our own truth, in the center of our own being, which is also the place where we meet God.

A few years ago a group did a study of the increasing trend of young people who are leaving Christianity. Books and articles were written. Leaders generated clever strategies to keep our kids from losing their faith. But I imagine many of these young people were right on schedule. In fact, a lot of people who were concerned about the trend had never left home themselves, so of course they would offer bad advice. There's no story without leaving home. Jesus would've never fulfilled his destiny if he didn't piss off his parents and siblings, who by the way thought he was crazy. Let's not forget that after preaching in his hometown, the people wanted to throw him off a cliff. Jesus never went home again.

So go ahead, run like hell.

I'm not trying to be overly prescriptive at this point. I'm highlighting a pattern. Only you can name what's become a burden that needs to be set down or left at the border crossing or taken off the camel's back. It's going to require a more dangerous trust of your own raw experience. Many Christians are taught to break trust with their own inner experience, and this is sometimes helpful advice when we're young. It's really hard to make it through adolescence when the voices in our heads are legion. But if we ever want to make it to adulthood we must start a lonely path back to the quiet inner whispers of our hearts. It's time to find out what's true in our real experience and not what is supposed to be true.

Those who are still pretty far from the border or busy loading up the camel's back—a place we all start—will not want us to leave and will not likely welcome our return. They will call it "losing faith," when the truth is, we are discovering faith.

Don't lose heart. This is the way it is when you courageously come down the ladder.

I've heard this call myself, at different times, with varying degrees of intensity. It's not likely to be a one-time thing. And I've also ignored this call. I made elaborate negotiations with the call, coming up with all kinds of justifications and compromises. I know you've heard it too, if you are still reading all this. You hear it in the wind, in a moonrise, in the laughter of a child, in a poem, in one line from a movie. Maybe it's a quiet whisper saying, "Just keep going" or a nudge saying, "Don't be afraid" or a question like Saint Francis's "Who are you God and who am I?" It feels like a "No" and a "Yes" at the same time.

As I approached forty, something kept hunting me down. I could feel it breathing down my neck more strongly than at any time in my life. I was watching my dad in the last stages of ALS. The ending of his life, and his roles, and the identity he formed, was a wakeup call to the way I was living. I didn't want to be a visitor in my own life. I began to have dreams that were puzzling and disturbing. Grief I could not explain welled up. I felt more at home in the woods than in the company of friends. I felt something shifting again, but not because I thought or believed anything in particular. It was time for a more radical authenticity, or simply honesty, even if it hurt. It was time to stand at the bottom of the ladder and say, "Now what?"

Mary Oliver became one of those echoes in the canyon, her words whispering to me in the wind. I heard the call in her poem, "The Journey." I wrote this poem on the white board in my church office. I read it out loud almost every day for a year. She speaks of a day when we finally know what we have to do. Every day I wondered, "What is she talking about?" And some days I feared I already knew what she was talking about.

The hints and guesses of what it's like to come down off the ladder of our first convictions, of our certainties, are all in this poem. She speaks clearly enough about what it's like to walk toward our unknowing. And most importantly she speaks to what we all want, a new recognition of our own true voice, keeping us company as we go further and further into the world, into the fullness of our own short and precious life.

I found a few small ways to say "yes" to the descent. It can be as small as paying attention to a poem, sleeping alone beneath the stars, giving away all your junk, walking out on a stifling relationship, or whatever feels alluring and scary at the same time.

9

COMING DOWN
FROM SINAI

The desert air and the warming sun no longer seemed so magical, so otherworldly. Sinai receded into every other mountain as the camel's saliva dried on my jacket. The Bedouin camps appeared plain and temporary while the young men sat around smoking and waiting for another night of making their strange living. Part of me wished I could sit alongside them, tea and cigarette in hand. Maybe it was just the daylight, but I saw a different mountain than the one I ascended.

I felt a little like Jacob who wrestled all night with God, or an angel, or himself, walking away with a limp. I could barely move my arm. The difference being that I received no new name. In fact, it seemed a little like I had lost my name, lost some identity marker, lost the spiritual Kent I was trying to prop up. Instead, I carried with me down the mountain a healthy embarrassment, even humiliation. My meaning-making self had grown quiet, the crunch of stones under my feet the only noise I noticed.

At the bottom of the mountain I wandered around the monastery waiting for this adventure to end, ready to go home to see my wife and daughter. I walked into a nondescript chapel. To my surprise, the room was full of human skulls, piled in a dusty heap. These were the bones of monks who had died here, trying to be near God, near to where God had supposedly revealed something. Unprepared for this visual assault, my first instinct was to walk out.

But I didn't move for a long time in this hall of death. Hundreds of skulls peered around the room through their vacant eye sockets. I breathed in the air, full of dust from these bones. On the one hand, these dead monks were resting with their brothers, piled up in a community of friends. How lucky to be gathered up like this. On the other hand, they seemed utterly alone, left to return to the earth from which they came. Why had the living piled up the dead like this? Who knows, but it felt like a calling card by the trail for all the tourists heading back to the so-called real world.

The message was obvious: "You're going to die."

This filled me with a mixture of sobriety and curiosity. My heart ached. All of us reach the same end, and too soon. This moment felt spiritually richer than any church service I ever attended. No singing, no sermons, just wind passing through open windows and the sun moving slowly along the barren floor. And a large pile of bones. I imagined my own skull somewhere in this junk pile of spiritual brothers. Instead of a heap of saints or heroes, it was just a heap of human beings. To see my own body twisted up with all the rest seemed like a fitting end to my failure to find God in the ways I had always tried to find God. Perhaps the universe was saying, "You'll be here before too long."

That chapel ended up being a good way to begin all the new wandering that ensued after Sinai. Some important part of me needed to be left behind, stripped off, unloaded. In fact, I think that much of my own first journey was about the quest for immortality and a super-spiritual-special-self on the top of a sacred mountain. But the second chapter is far more human. We all return to the bottom of the mountain to look into the face of our own mortality, one way or another. We can either do it now or when it feels too late.

This second faith is about becoming fully human rather than trying to get away from it. It's where we learn to embrace our own limitations, our tiny lives, and by doing so receive the infinite gift of participating in the great divine dance that is.

We're all dust-covered skulls in a heap of mysterious grace.

An Unknown Land

This actually fills me with hope. It's no longer about getting the spiritual life right, it's just about living the one messy and beautiful life I have, while I can. For me, it's about coming down the mountain.

Leaving my familiar evangelical home for an unknown land has been the greatest adventure of my life. And I've only begun to find my way into what feels like a new faith, so I'm no expert. Coming down Sinai, so-to-speak, took longer than the initial bruised descent. My own process of change hasn't been linear or straightforward, and as far as I can tell it's this way for everyone. I had to live with new questions and new experiences, fall down and get back up.

It's taken me a long time, for example, to know on the body-spirit-mind level that I am not a problem to God. Occasionally, I have flashbacks, but these are waning. It took me several years to let go of my attachments to the afterlife. After breaking up with the Bible, several times, it took time for a new love to grow between us. The ending of End Times didn't happen in a flash but only as I came to love the actual world and started to see God in all things. Coming down the ladder of religious knowledge took a while, and I slowly realized that the unknowing of God was a gift, not a curse. It was difficult to learn to trust that the truth was happening in my own life rather than located out there somewhere, in some other denomination, religion, creed, mountain, or special experience.

And I needed a lot of help, which I received from my Spiritual Director, my therapist, a couple of real friends, a generous spouse and partner, a few poets, and the healthy leveling of just being a parent. And being a parent, or even being around kids, is really good for starting a deeper spiritual adventure. When my kids say things like, "Who is God? Why go to church? Is hell a real place? Why do some people believe . . . ?" my spine straightens and I have the feeling something very important is in the air. The questions kids have is an invitation to explore what we really believe, or more likely what we think we believe, and what we no longer really believe. Kids expose the gap between our real experience and the "truths" we're supposed to pass on. Just pay attention the next time you swallow hard trying to explain something to a kid you're actually not sure you even know anything about. I probably should have given my own sermons to children before I ever gave them to adults.

To tell the truth, as best we can, doubts and misgivings admitted, is exposing but absolutely necessary for growing up. We tell this truth to ourselves first, before we ever trust it to another. It's a journey that's solitary, but not one in which loneliness has the final word. In fact, I found a lot less loneliness when I started to express my doubts and leave the confines of my own religious beliefs and church borders. In other words, I felt a darker loneliness trying to stuff what was naturally coming up than I did when I started getting more honest and real, come what may.

I thought I knew, at least a little bit, what the spiritual life was about. That's what paid my bills. But it stopped working. I thought it was about doing spiritual stuff, or talking about spiritual stuff, or believing stuff, the kind I heard about in church or read in spiritual books. But this is what I've learned: the spiritual life is my actual life.

I wish this were more sexy and cool, but it's really that plain. It's not something that we put on, or try on, or add to our real life. Sure, there are practices like prayer and meditation that can help us reconnect to what's real in our lives, but there's no division between the spiritual and everything

147

else. It's both an earnest prayer on an ancient mountain and the interruption of a singing hillside.

The sum total of our experiences, in all their messy glory, is where we live our spiritual lives. The walls come down between the sacred and secular. The car ride on the way to church, when we're yelling at our kids to shut up, is just as much our spiritual life as the music we pretend to like when we get there.

Who we are, right now, is enough. The life that we're living, right now, is enough.

This is a truth worth fighting for, worth the risk of believing. Many of us are walking out of church, in one way or another, or away from the protective shell of our held beliefs, because so many of the messages tell us that we're not enough. And as we walk out, we walk straight into the reality of our actual life.

God will not show up if we're good enough, right enough, spiritual enough, or somehow have the moral fortitude to ward off all ambiguity and messiness. God will not meet us on the top of a mountain, just because we make a big deal about going there. God is not actually hiding somewhere or waiting for us to play the game of beliefs in order to pass the eternal mega-test. On the bus ride back to Jerusalem from Sinai I listened for the millionth time to Radiohead's album, OK Computer. What a work of art. What a relief. Thank God for headphones. This was just as spiritual as my book of psalms, at least to me. The spirit of Mystery moved up and down my spine, I had goosebumps and tears, once again. All of it matters, all of it.

We have to learn to trust our real life again, the one we live in our body, spirit, and heart. In my view, to touch our raw experience requires passing through the eye of the needle, shedding a few unnecessary beliefs and attachments that protect us from such vulnerability. And the secret to this kind of spirituality is to pay attention to the ordinary. That's where God shows up.

A Spirituality of Ordinary Mystery

Somehow the ordinary never seems like enough. Recently I went on a three-day solo hike in the Utah desert. Sounds special enough. But I was actually worried that when I arrived in my spot, in the vast wilderness of Navajo sandstone, I would spend time wondering if it was just a little bit more beautiful over the next rise. This is a kind of mind virus. My constant search for a special place, or a special person, or a special job, or a special religion, or a special guru, so that I can finally live my really special life, keeps me from my actual life. On my solo, I stayed in one place for three days and nights, as I was instructed by my guide. The point became obvious over time: wake up to what is right in front of you!

The ordinary is all we have. I've spent too long searching for the extraordinary. This kind of search can send you the top of Mount Sinai, and that's still not enough. This kind of search sends you back down the mountain thinking, "Well, I'll have to do it again. Next time I'll make sure no one is there, no camels, no Bedouin, no tourists. Maybe there's another way up, up the backside. I'll come during the off season, then I'll really meet God." This cycle never ends. This kind of search is never over. We end up never seeing what's right in front of us. We all know people who are addicted to the next yoga retreat, the newest spiritual best-seller, the latest body cleanse, whatever. Never enough.

One of the most holy things we can do is accept the reality of our own lives. I'm preaching to myself, which is what I do in most of my sermons. I'm not saying we shouldn't work to change circumstances that are unhealthy or harmful. To change what we can change, and to accept what we cannot change, both require the spiritual practice of embracing our own ordinary reality.

It's like what Paula D'Arcy says, "God comes to you disguised as your life."[1]

My ordinary, plain, messy, unorganized, embarrassing life? My tiny moments of joy, that one flash of happiness, my unassuming little life, inside my own skin? The life that wakes up one morning convinced there's no God and by mid-afternoon experiences a divine mystery just watching my honeybees come and go? Yes. That one. I wonder how differently we'd live if we started getting really curious about what's disguised in our ordinary lives. To follow this curiosity about the ordinary is the best advice I can give right now.

Sometimes I meditate in the morning. Sometimes my kids walk in. "Dad's on his mediation pillow again," they say, rolling their eyes. More than once I've thought, "Well,

1. Paula D'Arcy, quoted by Richard Rohr in *Falling Upward: A Spirituality for the Two Halves of Life* (San Francisco: Jossey-Bass, 2011), 66.

that didn't work. I didn't get in my full twenty minutes. Guess I'm starting the day a little less spiritual." This is another mind virus. God just walked into the living room, and I didn't recognize her. All the prayer I need just came around the corner.

The spiritual life I'm talking about says, "This is really happening."

When I think about Sinai now, the God I was searching for, the divine encounter I desired, was already all around me. Reality was all around me. God was in the sum total of all the weirdness. A divine encounter was awaiting me in the shivering cold, in the first warmth of the sun, in the rented blanket, in the laughter of my fellow students, in a Snickers bar, in the hymn of the Beatles, in the ebb and flow of my own emotions, in my attempts and failures at a prayer life, in my tired body, in the silence of the desert—in other words, in my actual ordinary life.

Part of what's needed as we cross the border to a deeper faith is living the life we actually have. God is not off somewhere in a special place, or to be found doing a bunch of super-special spiritual things. In fact, God is not "out there." We cannot take seriously anymore a God up in heaven, really far away, a man in clouds, a superman being. Mystery, Reality, the Ground of All Being, the Great Spirit, are all slightly better names for the nameless found hidden in all things.

This sort of thing has a name. Some call it *panentheism.*[2]

2. I first heard this term a few years after Sinai from the Dominican Sisters of Marywood in Grand Rapids, Michigan.

This is a wordplay on pantheism, which means "God is all things." Pan-en-theism on the other hand means something like, "God is in everything" or "everything is in God." Or more simply, "All-in-God."

As the apostle Paul says, "In him we live and move and have our being." Paul was way ahead of his time on this one.

The divisions of sacred and secular were simply props to get things moving. Having a so-called "spiritual life" and a "secular life" was just an early way of trying to divide the world up to make sense of our existence. We call the church building the "house of God," until one day we realize the house of God is everywhere. The divisions dissolve. We say, like Jacob, "God was in this place and I didn't know it." Like Moses we take off our sandals in front of the burning shrubbery because we're already on holy ground. The desert itself is the temple. The whole earth is already holy.

Just living becomes a sacrament. Every living room is a temple. Every person is a high priest. Your body is the palace where God dwells. The tulip is the robe God is wearing. This is real faith, real spirituality, and real worship. And this is available to everyone, in his or her ordinary life, regardless of how good they think they are, or how sound or mixed-up their theological beliefs, or if they claim allegiance to, or disavow, organized religion.

This calls for a new sensitivity. We're invited to walk through the world as if everything is actually alive with the very life of God, which it is. The word of God is in the trees that give us shade, in the twisting river running through our towns, and in the thunderstorm that finally cools off the house we are borrowing from the bank, or really from God's own earthly body. This sensitivity brings the kind of aliveness our souls really crave.

"Here comes the sun," is a sacred hymn to the really real, which I call God. Little did I know how much my life would change when I first heard those voices in the middle of nowhere. Instead of ruining my divine encounter, they were a choir singing to the divine in all things. I just didn't have the ears to hear it yet.

Let me say it as plainly as I can. The future of our planet, our spiritual communities, our sanity, and our health depends upon waking up to the aliveness of God in all things. It's okay to become panentheists. It's time we fall in the love with the ordinary.

THE DIVINE GIFT OF LOSING FAITH

Coming back down the mountain was the beginning of a new faith adventure. To use biblical language, I had left Egypt and entered the wilderness. And more and more of us are leaving Egypt carrying nothing on our backs. So many of us are setting off to find the God we've been told about, but up on the mountain, we're experiencing massive disappointment. We get bitten, and the pain serves as a wakeup call. In the darkness, we start feeling our way toward a new way of being. We come down from Sinai, and we start a new kind of faith and a less churchy spirituality.

I am not claiming to know exactly what this new country is like. I'm still in the wilderness, having just left Egypt. But I believe the migration is happening, and I'm a part of it. Like the Israelites, many religious communities would rather stay in Egypt than be free. This seems inevitable, and maybe without the resistance, it would emerge much more slowly. The fight actually speeds it up. In other words, the institutional resistance to the breakdown of faith might actually be helping it fall apart, and to be reborn. So let's not be so hard on the institutions that "just don't get it." We don't really get it either. Resistance, tension, and unknowing are all part of this evolution.

There's historic precedent for this kind massive change in worldview. It's right inside the story of Jesus's followers. The disciples had to lose their religious worldview before Jesus started making sense to them. Their hopes and expectations for what the Messiah was going to be and do had to die. Jesus didn't take the throne or rule the city. And in fact, this collapse was essential for a deeper meaning to shine forth. Two things died on Good Friday: Jesus the man, and what his own followers needed him to be. And most of contemporary Christianity hasn't learned very much about the second death.

At first, the disciples turned back, probably to their old lives, their old religion, their old plans, and their old hopes for an external savior. They were probably singing something like, "Give me that old time religion," a favorite song of my childhood church world. According to the Gospels, a few days after Jesus's death, they were back to fishing, as if nothing had happened. It's possible they talked themselves out of the experiences they had with Jesus, like how we so easily forget a dream.

But as the disciples' messianic notions unraveled, the empty space created enough room for new images of Jesus to emerge. Grief opened a door. And rich and fruitful notions of Jesus emerged. The messiah of Jewish nationhood transformed into a symbol of belonging for all people. A Davidic-War-King became a warrior of nonviolent action. The rabbi became the Cosmic Christ. The body of Jesus became the living body of the church, a true second coming. The son of Joseph became the Son of all Men and all Women. These are all images from the New Testament. They reveal the adaptability of the Jesus movement, as different people worked it out in different ways.

In short, Jesus transformed into a resurrected and mystical Christ, an archetype of transformation, an image of Human-Divine unity, who embraced the love and the suffering of just being human, and who forgave the very enemies who strung him up. And the disciples followed in his way, the way of their own deaths and resurrections.

I don't think this requires throwing everything we've ever been taught about God in the trash. It's much less violent and not so much a matter of willpower. It's more like we cooperate with what's already happening, with the unraveling in our own lives, the acute places of suffering or passion, the places we've been bitten. It happened to me this way. It happened climbing mountains, giving sermons, reading books, raising kids, asking questions, going to church, not going to church, finding like-minded friends, success, failures, spending time in the woods, flashes of clarity, and moments of confusion. It was like a death and resurrection, which is the point of the Jesus story. Paradoxically, this kind of transformation is chosen and not chosen. It's gift and invitation. There's no need to work out the difference.

When this kind of change starts happening, it's not confined to a religion or even a belief system. More and more I'm finding how little belief has to do with it. Nor is it explicitly anti-religious. It's not about hating the past, or the doctrines, or the tribes, or our churches. But sooner or later the right religion, or the right words, stops mattering all that much. This is where I find myself. I can go to a Good Friday service, which is all about the confusion of death and the longing for new life, and feel at home. I can also stay at home, with a few friends, or with my kids, and at those moments, going to church would be pointless.

I don't know if in the future fewer and fewer people will be in church. It seems like we're heading that way. Church was never a building or an institution in the early days anyway. But whether or not we're inside a church on a Sunday morning or if we're doctrinally sound won't really matter all that much. If some version of church helps us experience more of our given wholeness, if we get a sense there's no canyon between us and God, if our humanity deepens, if it creates space for doubt and even room for our own shadowy stuff we don't want to face, then by all means, keep going. But if we're experiencing the opposite, it's bad for our health.

When I lived in Israel I went to see one of my professors

to get help with a paper. We'd become friends. After some academic chatter the conversation turned personal. I'd been reading Thomas Merton and we talked about his radical move to the monastery. I had recently read *The Seven Story Mountain* and fallen in love with his passionate quest for God. I talked openly about wanting to convert to something. I was having one of my regular existential freak-out sessions. He walked over to his floor-to-ceiling shelves and pulled down a book. He said, "Here, read this. It's a collection of Thomas Merton's writings shaped into prayers."

I took the book home, sat down on my bed, and read the opening prayer.

Dear Lord God, I have no idea of where I am going. I do not see the road ahead of me. I cannot know for certain where it will end. Nor do I really know myself, and the fact that I think I am following your will does not mean I am actually doing so. But I believe the desire to please you does in fact please you. And I hope I have that desire in all that I'm doing. I hope that I will not do anything apart from that desire. I know that if I do this you will lead me by the right road, though I may know nothing about it. Therefore I will trust you always, though I may seem to be lost and in the shadow of death. I will not fear, for you are ever with me, and you will not leave me to face my perils alone.[3]

3. Thomas Merton, *New Seeds of Contemplation* (New York: New Directions, 1962), 227.

I cried my eyes out in relief.

I don't quite know the path. I've been bitten, and I suppose I'll be bitten again. The classic Jonah-Jesus pattern is a week of massive failures, followed by a death, then silence, all before the rumors of new life start sprouting. But if we go this way, we'll be asked to trust our own experiences. We'll be asked to trust in the goodness of the universe despite evidence to contrary. We'll be asked to check our beliefs at the border and get ready to discover something new, that we come to learn ourselves. But we'll also come alive as never before.

I'm now grateful that the camel bit me. I learned just how important it is to pay attention to the places I've been bitten, to the parts in me that are unraveling, to my ordinary and real life.

What I didn't know is that coming down the mountain turned out to be as important as ascending.

Leaving behind my things at the border was as important as first collecting them.

Unloading the camel turned out to be as needed as weighing it down with my first beliefs, images, and ideas about God.

But now the camel is a little lighter.

I'm less certain about things but also more open.

I find hints and guesses about the mystery of God in the most ordinary places in my life.

I have started to leave church, leave my old way of being in the world, and find God, an unknown and nameless God at that. It's been a wild undoing, but very good.